The Science of Accelerated Learning:
Advanced Strategies for Quicker Comprehension, Greater Retention, and Systematic Expertise

By Peter Hollins,
Author and Researcher at
petehollins.com

Table of Contents

Introduction

Learning has never come easy for me, which explains my standing as a mediocre student K-12 and through college.

Even my parents seemed to intuitively know this, as they started to tell me about my "street smarts" and how good I was with my hands. I assumed this was just so they could find something to praise me about, because they didn't really have the opportunity to do so with my grades.

It was never something I struggled with or felt bad about like other kids might. I suppose other kids might have seen other people at the top of the class and become frustrated and jealous. I just felt that everyone had something to contribute in their own way and that grades weren't necessarily a measure of my own worth.

I know, that's pretty insightful for a child. But in many ways, it was also incredibly misguided.

It turns out I was right about grades not being important. Life *is* partially about whom you know, but once you get there, it starts becoming a meritocracy. The concept of learning—the ability to understand, recall, and use new knowledge—well, that's something that truly begins to matter and can make all the difference in your career, relationships, and happiness. In fact, it becomes the backbone of where you end up, though you might get a leg up on where you start.

If you can learn quickly, you can effectively walk the walk before anyone catches on that you were bluffing the entire time. You can discover opportunities you would never see otherwise if you were stuck in something. And you generally have the ability to steer your life in whatever direction you want because your ability to learn is your only barrier to entry!

This was never more apparent to me than at my first job. I had a coworker named John, and I started a few weeks before he did. It soon become apparent that he had lied on his resume and faked his way through his interview, because he had no idea what his duties were supposed to be or how to use the industry-standard software that we were all supposed to be proficient in.

At first, I was angry and wanted to see justice done. But then a funny thing happened—he was an *immensely* fast learner. He had Post-it notes all over his desk had notepads full of notes, and he always seemed to be writing sets of three-step instructions for himself. It was impressive for me to see his drive toward learning, and within months, he was performing at right about my own level of proficiency with everything he had lacked before.

Sure, he may have faked his way in, but at this point, there was no practical difference between me and him. He had learned how to do our job in record time and stayed at the company for years afterward. You could call this a sobering epiphany for how I thought about the *processes* and *value* of learning.

Processes: It can't be that hard, and there must be tried and true systems people use to learn better. After all, the kids that had better grades than I did definitely weren't all smarter than me, right?

Value: Wow, learning can unlock so many doors. I had no idea. It applies to way more than work and probably to my hobbies and daily life, too. Learning will get me where I want to be.

So what exactly is learning (not a technical definition)? Learning is how you create the life you want. Learning is the only way to create a better version of yourself. Learning is one of the most fundamental skills you can possess because if you don't have it, how will your existence change or improve?

Welcome to *accelerated learning*, where you can finally learn how to learn.

Chapter 1. Fertile Conditions to Learning

How do we learn?

It seems like such a simple question, but decades of scientific literature tend to disagree with that notion. We may simply consider learning an activity we just started as a baby with no preparation. In our school years, we were the receptacles for a constant flow of information and experiences. And in most traditional settings, instructors measured how well we learned by how well we repeated the information back to them.

We had no choice in the matter and simply went along with what was presented to us.

This data accumulation and regurgitation almost suggest that learning is an automated process that we can only monitor, not control. In truth, there are factors, limitations, and conditions that affect our ability to learn. Understanding these elements can help you avoid mistakes and accelerate your learning. This book uses scientific principles and methods that will help you learn in a way that works best for you.

All mental activities, including learning, are influenced by internal and external factors and conditions. Some factors we can control; others we have to overcome or work around. This first chapter discusses the scientific principles that drive our learning abilities and some of the best practices we can use to expand learning capacity. In other words, we must create fertile conditions for learning; otherwise, we are sabotaging ourselves.

You wouldn't try to learn to ski in a desert, would you?

The Human Attention Span

One of the first conditions to learning you must take into account is your attention span. Since 2006, the nonprofit group Technology, Entertainment and Design—universally known as TED—has produced a series of online videos featuring influential speakers and leaders from all walks of business and life. TED Talks have become a viral source of sharing ideas and spreading inspiration.

A big key to the success of TED Talks is their brevity: all of them are capped at 18 minutes. TED curator Chris Anderson explained, "It is long enough to be serious and short enough to hold people's attention. . . . By forcing speakers who are used to going on for 45 minutes to bring it down to 18, you get them to really think about what they want to say. What is the key point they want to communicate?"

The overwhelming majority of Hollywood movies run no longer than 150 minutes; in 2016, half of them ran two hours or less. Movies are easier to sit through because they're essentially passive: with the visuals taken care of, we don't have to use extra brain energy to imagine them. TED talks, on the other hand, are more active, participatory, and dense, with few visual stimulants besides one person moving around on a stage. They have to be shorter. There are no accidents here; these are all intentional to cater to the human attention span and be as impactful as possible.

But TED Talks and movies both consume brainpower, though at different rates. At some point in the brain gets fatigued and has to take a break to recharge, whether it's through distraction or relaxation. Whether it's a one-hour lecture or a three-hour film, that mental weariness eventually sets in.

Studies have suggested that the attention span of a healthy adult is, on average, 15 minutes long. Other studies (Microsoft Corporation) assert that our immediate attention span—a single block of concentration—has fallen to an average of *8.25 seconds*. That's less than that of a goldfish, which have been shown to be able to maintain focus for a near-eternity of nine seconds.

You can only learn as much as you can pay attention to; therefore, much research in the area of learning and retention focuses on the aspect of time.

Ellen Dunn of Louisiana State University's Center for Academic Success suggests between 30 and 50 minutes is the ideal length for learning new material. "Anything less than 30 is just not enough," Dunn said, "but anything more than 50 is too much information for your brain to take in at one time." After the completion of one session, you should take a five- to ten-minute break before starting another.

In the 1950s, researchers William Dement and Nathaniel Kleitman found that the human body generally operates in 90-minute cycles, whether awake or asleep. This pattern is called the "ultradian rhythm." The start of each cycle is defined as a period of "arousal," ramping up to a mid-period of high performance before finally decelerating in a period of "stress." Understanding how the 90-minute rhythm cycle works in the context of the greater 24-hour rhythm—the "circadian rhythm"—can help us predict how we'll function over the course of a day and how we can plan around it for peak performance.

All these examples and studies point to one primary strategy for improving our learning: breaking it down into smaller chunks of time because a flood of information will simply not make it into our heads.

Learning Over Short Bursts of Time

By segmenting our learning activities according to blocks of time, we give the brain enough time off to reset and reenergize and enable ourselves to retain more information over longer periods. It's therefore a good idea to start a new learning routine by simply setting up a schedule.

Long-term planning. At the beginning of a semester, online course, or research project, block out your schedule to set up a studying regimen. You can do this easily with a free online calendar program from virtually all Internet providers or with a paper calendar or whiteboard.

Consider what times of day you tend to get the most accomplished—some of us start the day in high-performance mode, while others are classic night owls. Just make sure to leave ample time for sleep and eating. In fact, there is a scientific basis for whether you are more productive at night or in the morning, summed up by the terms morning larks and night owls.

If you're really tuned in to your brain and body, you can get a bit more granular with your scheduling by applying the 90-minute cycle to the calendar—for instance, 90-minute blocks that account for breaks and fatigue. This requires a little more careful introspection and monitoring, but if you can narrow down an even more specific time when your performance abilities are higher, you can fine-tune your learning agenda even further.

Learning blocks. You can adapt the 30–50-minute study session as dictated by the LSU study for your own purposes. Remember that 30 minutes is enough to make the study session substantial enough and that going over 50 puts undue pressure on your brain. So within your weekly time block, make sure to schedule an attendant break after your core learning time.

Again, adjust it to what you know your system can handle: maybe it's 50 minutes with a 10-minute break or 45 minutes with a 15-minute break. The study session can go down all the way to 30 minutes if absolutely necessary. You can use the renowned Pomodoro clock, which is commonly used for work productivity—25 minutes of activity followed by five minutes of total removal from that activity. The specific amount of time is not set hard and fast; whatever it is, it just needs to be a time frame easy enough for you to stick through on a regular basis.

Just ask yourself how you might cater to the attention span of a goldfish or even a child.

Our adult minds are not so different as we might like to think.

Concepts Before Facts, Understanding Before Memory

Researcher Roger Säljö found in 1979 that we tend to view the act of learning in several ways, but it can generally be boiled down into two rough categories: *surface* learning and *deep* learning. Surface learning relates to gaining knowledge, facts, and memorization; deep learning refers to abstracting meaning and understanding reality.

The use of the words "surface" and "deep" might imply that the latter is better in all situations than the former, but that's not always true. Some things are best learned by memorization rather than additionally searching for some "meaning" to contextualize those things. If I gave you a list of 30 random items and asked you to remember them, it probably wouldn't help to ransack your brain trying to find a pattern or relationship between each item. It would waste your time when the task at hand is simple information retention.

But more often than not, rote memorization serves to isolate facts rather than connect them. It establishes facts as single pieces of information, and without a grounding context or relationship to a greater concept, it doesn't anchor what you learn. Sometimes this is fine, but as a consequence, what you learn slips out of your short-term memory quite easily.

The overwhelming majority of things that can be learned have some kind of pattern—hidden or obvious. These patterns, typically, are what you most care about learning. Without these patterns, frankly, what you learn wouldn't be useful anyway. Patterns make concepts useful. Without them, concepts have very limited or temporary relevance and would therefore not be important to study in the first place.

A typical course of study contains a mix of big ideas with few details. In that setting, it's always the best idea to start with the big ideas—the overarching concepts that link the little details together.

The primary reason is that many small details take on a random quality at first, but when seen through the lens of the larger concept, they fit together and form a context. That makes them easier for the brain to recognize and remember.

In fact, you can often forgo a lot of memorization, because the concepts themselves often serve to explain the facts. Instead of attempting to memorize by rote means, following the concept through to its conclusion will reveal the facts as you go along. Like subheadings in an outline, they fall into place under the appropriate headings— it's a logical progression. If you understand the governing principles around something, the facts follow organically.

For example, if you were studying about the history of Miranda rights in the United States, you could memorize all the key players: the Supreme Court Justices, the lawyers, and the names of the plaintiffs and defendants. You could memorize the dates in the case. You could memorize the vote counts from all the courts involved in the suit and the appeals. You could memorize the names of cases that came afterward. You could even write down the contents of the Miranda rights ("You have the right to remain silent," etc.).

None of those facts would have any relevance by themselves, and we'd have no reason to keep them in memory. Emphasizing the larger concepts surrounding the Miranda rule—defendant's rights, police procedure, or landmark Supreme Court cases—help to funnel the facts as they come up. In this context, the brain is more likely to retain the information it actually needs to know about the subject. You would be able to essentially predict the facts with a reasonable degree of accuracy once you understand the underlying concepts and how they interact.

This is known as *concept learning*. It shows us how to categorize and discriminate items according to certain critical attributes. It entails pattern recall and integration of new examples and ideas. And rather than being a mechanical technique of grinding memorization, concept learning is something that must be constructed and cultivated.

Using Concept Learning in Daily Life. Applying the concept method to learning and developing new skills, even outside of the classroom or study hall environment, can help derive new meaning and, by logical extension, even improve how we perform certain tasks or jobs.

Cooking is an easy example. Standard practice is that learning a new recipe involves following a list of ingredients and a set of instructions. If you're making a tomato sauce for pasta, you can look up a popular recipe on the Internet and have it nearby as you prepare it. You can repeat this exercise as often as you like, and eventually you'll probably know the steps well enough to repeat it without a guide.

But understanding the *point* of each step isn't something that comes through in the instructions. They generally don't say *why* you sweat onions and garlic first, *why* you bring the sauce to a boil, or *why* you let it simmer for a time. Understanding that sweating the onions and garlic builds a flavor base, that boiling the sauce distributes the ingredients, and that simmering them bonds the flavors together gives you a better handle on the process of your preparation.

Most importantly, understanding those concepts makes it easier to recognize and use the techniques in other, completely different dishes: soups, chili, gravy, and even basic broth and stock. Going even further, learning the particulars of the exact scientific processes could open the door to *entirely* different foods that aren't liquid-based—in other words, any food you can think of. If you simply know which flavors tend to conflict and which tend to complement, you'll be way ahead of the chef who memorizes recipes.

This template is sneakily easy to replicate. A small business owner figuring a tax budget is better served knowing the concepts of taxation and how they're distributed. A musician who understands how rhythm works in the context of a song better knows how to program a drum machine. A chess player gets more mileage from comprehending the differences between overall strategies rather than learning where each piece can move. Even a clothes launderer makes fewer mistakes and ruins less clothing by learning how cold water and hot water affect colors in variant ways.

You can learn the particulars of any task and even perform it suitably a few times. But knowing the principles and ideas that link them together is a more effective way to preserve and retain those facts or skills. When the time comes to learn something new, you may very well be able to frame that new knowledge with concepts you've already nailed down.

Learning heuristics is very similar to the act of concept learning (Barsalou, 1991, 1992). Heuristics describes a pattern of thought or behavior that organizes categories of information and the relationships among them. It takes our preconceived notions or ideas of the world and uses them as a means for interpreting and classifying new information.

For example, there are ways you might act at a birthday party that you wouldn't at a funeral (and, we'd hope, the other way around). The "codes" you follow for how you'd handle and behave in each situation, and any other occasions, are ordered within a heuristic. Establishing and understanding the heuristic rules for whatever you're about to learn is always helpful.

Another great way to learn concepts is the Feynman technique, which we'll discuss in a later chapter.

Aim to Be Frustrated (Yes, Really)

In competitive situations, we tie accomplishment with success: winning, positive outcomes, and finding solutions. But in learning, a key component in achievement is *failing*.

"Productive failure" is an idea identified by Manu Kapur, a researcher at the National Institute of Education in Singapore. The philosophy builds on the learning paradox, wherein *not* arriving at the desired effect is as valuable as prevailing, if not more.

Kapur said that the accepted model of instilling knowledge—giving students structure and guidance early and continuing support until the students can get it on their own—might not be the best way to actually promote learning. Although that model intuitively makes sense, according to Kapur it's best to let students flounder by themselves without outside help.

Kapur conducted a trial with two groups of students. In one group, students were given a set of problems with "scaffolding"—full instructional support from teachers on-site. The second group was given the same problems but received no teacher help whatsoever. Instead, the second group of students had to collaborate to find the solutions.

The "scaffolded" group was able to solve the problems correctly, while the group left to itself was not. But without instructional support, this second group was forced to do deeper dives into the problems by working together. They generated ideas about the nature of the problems and speculated on what potential solutions might look like. They tried to understand the root of the problems and what methods were available to solve them.

The two groups were then tested on what they had just learned, and the results weren't even close. The group without teacher assistance *significantly outperformed* the other group. The group that did not solve the problems discovered what Kapur deemed a "hidden efficacy" in failure: they nurtured a deeper understanding of the structure of the problems through group investigation and process.

The second group may not have solved the problem itself, but it learned more about the aspects of the problem. Going forward, when those students encounter a new problem on another test, they're able to use the knowledge they generated through their trial more effectively than the passive recipients of an instructor's expertise.

Consequently, Kapur asserted that the important parts of the second group's process were their miscues, mistakes, and fumbling. When that group made the active effort to learn by itself, it retained more knowledge needed for future problems.

Three conditions, Kapur said, make productive failure an effective process:

- Choose problems that "challenge, but do not frustrate."

- Give learners the chance to explain and elaborate their processes.

- Allow learners to compare and contrast good and bad solutions.

Struggling with something is a definite condition to learning, though it requires discipline and a sense of delayed gratification.

Helping Children to . . . Fail?

The notion of productive failure can also be seen in strategies for child-raising. Does intentionally letting our children fail actually make learning easier for them?

Judith Locke of the Queensland University of Technology said that "over-parenting" might keep our children safe and supported but could impede their growing processes. Locke observed that parents who raised their children in a state of helplessness were destined to lead anxiety-ridden adulthoods. Parents who were overly responsive to their children's needs restricted their children's ability to solve problems on their own and hampered the development of emotions they need to cope with future setbacks and failures.

In a way, we over-parent *ourselves*. We push ourselves not to fail, work too hard to achieve the desired outcome, and get frustrated when we get stuck or fall short. How can we, so to speak, let failing work for us?

Get your brain into "growth" mode. When we believe that we have all we need to accomplish whatever we want, we're setting ourselves up for disappointment when our process goes awry. This is because we think our abilities are fixed—if we can't succeed based on what we already know or can do, we never will. That makes our disappointments more profound and corrosive.

So at the beginning of a project that seems unfamiliar, we need to tell our brain that we're in learning mode. We need to establish that one of our main takeaways from this undertaking will be new *knowledge*, not just an immediately successful outcome. Reframe your expectations to make the learning as important as the result—*more* important, if possible.

Document your process. Companies use "paper trails" (literally or digitally) to determine points or events that altered an outcome. When you're in the weeds of a new project, keeping your own trail will help you learn new knowledge and refine your processes for later times.

In addition to whatever tools you're using for a project, set up a means to make a diary or journal for what you discover on the way. Set this diary up any way you want, whether it's a paper notepad, word processing or text software, the audio recorder on your smartphone, or whatever your preference. Document your process the way a chef would write down the steps of a recipe or a detective would remark upon evidence in an investigation.

These notes can be the kernels of knowledge that will come in handy in future situations— even if what you're using them for now ends in failure. The ideas they generate might seem small, especially if they end up not working. But when we use these kernels to solve future problems, their value increases. You may not notice any insight on a day-to-day basis, but when you compare weeks or months of progress, the difference may be startling.

Use your failures to plan next steps. If you've documented your process and diagnosed where something went wrong, then turn those evaluations into plans apart from your project.

For example, let's say you're planting a vegetable garden for the first, noting the steps and techniques you use along the way, and when it's time to harvest, some of your plants didn't come out the way they were supposed to. Was it because you used the wrong soil? Use your resources to find *why* that soil was wrong and what it needs to look like. Was the failed plant too close to another? Learn techniques for maximizing placement within a small space.

Or in a slightly more common situation, let's say your sales results fell short of projections. If you found a mistake that led to an over-estimate, find online information on how to set up your spreadsheet to avoid those errors. If your sales "game" was off, find workshops that can help improve your pitch or increase your interpersonal skills with clients. If you just didn't have enough clients, learn how to make your professional network broader and more potent.

Expect, but don't succumb to, frustration. Chances are you'll come across a moment or two of defeat in your process, along with the temptation to give up. You may even sense this before you start, which can lead to crippling anxiety that can hover over your work.

Anticipating frustration in advance is just good planning—but you also have to plan how to deal with it. Sketch out a plan or idea on how to alleviate frustration when it happens—most often, this will be taking a break from the situation to recharge and getting some momentary distance from the problem. Quite often, the mere act of pausing allows for objectivity to seep in, letting you see the hang-up more clearly. But in any case, it will abate the most immediate anxieties you're feeling and give you the chance to approach the issue from a more relaxed frame of mind.

Why are we even bothering to tackle preconditions to effective learning? Because many people dive right into learning without understanding what works on a psychological and even physical level. Many others think that effective learning is measured by the number of hours spent on a task, but we all have our limitations, and working within those bounds will only accelerate your learning. You can't outwork your attention span or commitment to rote memorization.

Takeaways to Accelerate Your Learning

1. The human attention span is significantly shorter than you would ever assume, so you must cater to it by learning in smaller blocks of time. You must also factor rest and recovery time into your learning because, like an athlete, this is where the difference is made

2. Seek to prioritize underlying concepts over information. Rote memorization is rarely the most helpful kind of learning. If you learn underlying concepts first, the

information can actually be predicted to some degree.

3. Fail, struggle, and be frustrated. It's this type of fixation that makes cements information and concepts into your memory. In essence, taking the hard way and avoiding the shortcut is how effective learning takes place. The shortcut creates learned helplessness.

Chapter 2. Memory Retention

Memory, of course, is heavily related to learning. If memory is a storage system that exists within specific neural pathways, then learning is about changing neural pathways to adapt one's behavior and thinking to the emergence of new information. They depend on each other because the goal of learning is to assimilate new knowledge into memory, and memory is useless without the ability to learn more.

Memorization is how we store and retrieve information for use (essentially the process of learning), and there are three steps to creating a memory. An error in any of these steps will result in knowledge that is not effectively converted to memory—a weak memory or the feeling of "I can't remember his name, but he was wearing purple . . ."

1. Encoding
2. Storage
3. Retrieval

Encoding is the step of processing information through your senses. We do this constantly, and you are doing it right now. We encode information both consciously and subconsciously through all of our senses. If you are reading a book, you are using your eyes to encode information, but how much attention and focus are you actually using? The more attention and focus you devote to an activity, the more conscious your encoding becomes—otherwise, it can be said that you subconsciously encode information, like listening to music at a café or seeing traffic pass you by at a red traffic light.

How much focus and attention you devote also determines how strong the memory is and, consequently, whether that memory only makes it to your short-term memory or if it passes through the gate to your long-term memory. If you are reading a book while watching television, your encoding is probably not too deep or strong.

Storage is the next step after you've experienced information with your senses and encoded it. What happens to the information once it passes through your eyes or ears? There are three choices for where this information can go, and they determine whether it's a memory that you will consciously know exists. There are essentially three memory systems: sensory memory, short-term memory, and long-term memory.

The last step of the memory process is **retrieval**, which is when we actually use our memories and can be said to have learned something. You might be able to recall it from nothing, or you might need a cue to bring the memory up. Other memories might only be memorized in a sequence or as part of a whole, like reciting the ABCs and then realizing you need to sing it to remember how it goes. Usually, however much attention you devoted to the storage and encoding phases of memory determines just how easy it is to retrieve those memories. Most of the learning process isn't necessarily focused on retrieval—it's focused on the storage aspect and what you can do to force information from sensory and short-term areas into long-term areas.

Think about when you cram for a test. You want information you experience to be in your brain for perhaps 24 hours, which means it has to exist beyond short-term memory and certainly beyond sensory memory. You might not care if you remember this information about the French Revolution at the end of the year, so you will reach a level of attention and focus that will push the information into the hazy area between short-term and long-term memory. In reality, what's happening is that you will rehearse the information enough to make a very faint imprint on your long-term memory.

Accelerating your learning, in a sense, is the same as improving your memory capacity and how absorbent your memory is—the more sponge-like, the better.

Forgetting

However, learning is both the process of improving memory while also getting better at *not forgetting*. Why do we forget? Why can't we remember this fact? How did we ever let something slip from our brains?

As you have read, forgetting is usually a failure or shortcoming in the storage process—the information you want only makes it to short-term memory, not long-term. The problem isn't that you can't find the information in your brain; it's that the information wasn't embedded strongly enough in your brain to begin with.

Sometimes it's easier to think about forgetting as a failure in learning. There are generally three different ways you retrieve or access your memories:

1. Recall
2. Recognition
3. Relearning

Recall is when you remember a memory without external cues. It's when you can recite something on command in a vacuum—for example, looking at a blank piece of paper and then writing down the capitals of all of the countries of the world. When you can recall something, you have the strongest memory of it. You have either rehearsed it enough or attached enough significance to it so that it is an incredibly strong memory within your long-term memory. Of course, because recall represents the strongest level of memory, it's also typically the toughest to achieve. It would typically require hours of rehearsal or study to get anywhere close to this. When we study, we want information to enter this realm, but we will usually settle for the next type of memory retrieval.

Recognition is when you can conjure up your memory in the presence of an external cue. It's when you might not be able to remember something by pure recall, but if you get a small clue or reminder, you will be able to remember it. For example, you might not be able to remember all of the capitals of the world, but if you got a clue such as the first letter of the capital or something that rhymes with the capital, it would be fairly easy to state it. When we cram information, this is typically what we end up with. This is also how mnemonics and similar memory devices work. We know we aren't able to definitively store and recall so many pieces of information with a massive amount of rehearsal, so we work on chunking information into easily recognizable cues.

Relearning is undoubtedly the weakest form of recall. It occurs when you are relearning or reviewing information and it takes you less effort each subsequent time. For example, if you read a list of country capitals on Monday and it takes you 30 minutes, it should take you 15 minutes the next day, and so on. Unfortunately, this is where we mostly lie on a daily basis. We might be familiar with a concept, but we haven't committed enough of it to memory to avoid essentially relearning it when we look at it again. This is what happens when we are new to a topic or we've forgotten most of it already. When you're in the relearning stage, you essentially haven't taken anything past the barrier of short-term memory into long-term memory.

The Forgetting Curve

Not only are we fighting weak encoding or storage in our quest for learning, we are also fighting the brain's natural tendency to forget as soon as possible.

This is encapsulated by the *forgetting curve*, a concept pioneered by psychologist Hermann Ebbinghaus. Below is a picture of the forgetting curve, courtesy of Wranx.com.

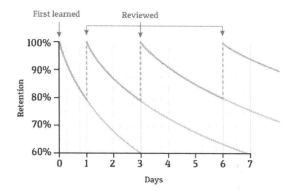

Typical Forgetting Curve for Newly Learned Information

This shows the rate of memory decay and forgetting over time if there is no attempt to move this information into long-term memory. If you read something about the French Revolution on Monday, then it's typically expected that you will remember only half of it after four days and retain as little as 30% at around a week's time. If you don't review what you've learned, it's very likely you will only retain 10% of what you learned about the French Revolution. However, if you review and rehearse it, you can see in the graph above how you will retain and memorize more over time. You will bump the retention level back up to 100%, and then the graph will start to become shallower, indicating less decay.

The goal with the knowledge of the forgetting curve is to make the curve shallower—to make it resemble a horizontal line as much as possible. That would indicate very little decay, and doing that requires constant review and rehearsal.

Ebbinghaus found patterns for memory loss and isolated two simple factors that affected the forgetting curve. First, the rate of decay was significantly blunted if the memory was strong and powerful and had personal significance to the person. Second, the amount of time and how old the memory was determined how quickly and severely it decayed. This suggests there is little we can do about forgetting other than to come up with tactics to assign personal significance to information and rehearse more often.

As you can see, forgetting isn't as simple as having something on the tip of your tongue or rummaging through the stores of your brain. There are very specific processes that make it a near-miracle that we actually retain as much as we do.

Being able to recall information is always the goal, but more realistically, we should be shooting for recognition and to learn how to expertly use cues and hints in our daily lives. I may not be able to recite the lyrics of my favorite songs, but I can sure remember them if I hear the melody.

Retrieval Practice

So how can we use this knowledge about our memories to be more effective learners? There is one major technique that applies the fickle nature of memory: *retrieval practice*.

We typically consider learning something we absorb—something that goes *into* our brains: the teacher or textbook spits facts, data, equations, and words out at us, and we just sit there and collect them. It's merely accumulation—a very *passive* act.

This kind of relationship with learning returns knowledge that we don't retain for very long because, even though we *get* it, we don't *do* much with it. For best results, we have to make learning an *active* operation.

That's where retrieval practice comes into play. Instead of putting more stuff *in* our brains, retrieval practice helps us take knowledge *out* of our brains and put it to use. That seemingly small change in thinking dramatically improves our chances of retaining and remembering what we learn. Everyone remembers flashcards from childhood days. The fronts of the cards had math equations, words, science terms, or images, and the backs had the "answer"—the solution, definition, explanation, or whatever response the student is expected to give.

The idea of flashcards sprouts from a strategy called *retrieval practice*. This approach is neither new nor very complicated: it's simply recalling information you've already learned (the back of the flashcard) when prompted by a certain image or depiction (the front).

Retrieval practice is one of the best ways to increase your memory and fact retention. But even though its core is quite simple, actually using retrieval practice isn't quite as straightforward as just passively using flashcards or scanning over notes we've taken. Rather, retrieval practice is an active skill: truly struggling, thinking, and processing to finally get to the point of recalling that information without clues—much of what we've discussed already in this book that accelerates learning.

Pooja Agarwal researched pupils taking middle school social studies over the course of a year and a half ending in 2011. The study aimed to determine how regularly scheduled, uncounted quizzes—basically, retrieval practice exercises—benefitted the ability to learn and retain.

The class teacher didn't alter their study plan and simply instructed as normal. The students were given regular quizzes—developed by the research team—on class material with the understanding that the results would *not* count against their grades.

These quizzes only covered about a third of the material covered by the teacher, who also had to leave the room while the quiz was being taken by the students. This was so the teacher had no knowledge of what subjects the quizzes covered. During class, the teacher taught and reviewed the class as usual, without knowing which parts of the instruction were being asked on the quizzes.

The results of this study were measured during end-of-unit exams and were quite dramatic. Students scored one full grade level higher on the material the quizzes covered— the one-third of what the whole class covered—than the questions *not* covered on the no-stakes quizzes. The mere act of being occasionally tested, with no pressure to get all the answers right to boost their overall grades, actually helped students learn better.

Agarwal's study also provided insight on what kind of questions helped the most. Questions that required the student to actually recall the information from scratch yielded more success than multiple-choice questions, in which the answer could be recognized from a list, or true/false questions. The active mental effort to remember the answer, with no verbal or visual prompt, improved the students' learning and retention.

Using Retrieval Practice in Our Lives

The principal benefit of retrieval practice is that it encourages an *active* exertion of effort rather than the passive seepage of external information. When we learn something once and then actually *do* something else to reinforce our learning, it has more of an effect than merely reviewing notes or re-reading passages in books.

The knowledge that we store in our memory is activated when it's called out. Retrieval practice stimulates that movement and makes it easier to learn and retain new understandings. If we pull concepts *out* of our brain, it's more effective than just continually trying to put concepts *in*. The learning comes from taking what's been added to our knowledge and bringing it out at a later time.

We mentioned flashcards at the top of this section, and how they're an offshoot of retrieval practice. But flashcards are not, in and of themselves, the strategy: you *can* use them and still not be conducting true retrieval practice.

Many students use flashcards somewhat inactively: they see the prompt, answer it in their heads, tell themselves they know it, flip over to see the answer, and then move on to the next one. Turning this into *practice*, however, would be taking a few seconds to actually recall the answer and, at best, say the answer out loud before flipping the card over. The difference seems slight and subtle, but it's important. Students will get more advantages from flashcards by actually retrieving and vocalizing the answer before moving on.

In real-world situations—where there's usually not an outside teacher, premade flashcards, or other assistance—how can we repurpose what we learn for retrieval practice? One good way is to expand flashcards to make them more "interactive."

The flashcards in our grade-school experiences, for the most part, were very one-note. You can adapt the methodology of flashcards for more complex, real-world applications or self-learning by taking a new approach to what's on the back of the cards, as suggested by writer Rachel Adragna.

When you're studying material for work or class, make flashcards with concepts on the front and definitions on the back. After completing this task, make another set of cards that give "instructions" on how to reprocess the concept for a creative or real-life situation. Here's an example:

- "Rewrite this concept in plain English."

- "Write a movie or novel plot that demonstrates this concept."

- "Use this concept to describe a real-life event."

- "Describe the *opposite* of this concept."

- "Draw a picture of this concept."

The possibilities are, as they say, limitless in how you can seek retrieval. Using these exercises extracts more information about the concept that you produce yourself. Placing them in context of a creative narrative or expression will help you understand them when they come up in real life. Our memories are fickle, and they like to play tricks on us by design, but they can be molded to our advantage in learning more quickly.

Takeaways to Accelerate Your Learning

1. Memory is what we are trying to change when we learn, and it is composed of encoding, storage, and retrieval. There are numerous pitfalls in each of those stages that sabotage our learning.

2. We use our memories by recalling, recognizing, or relearning information, but we also have to contend with the forgetting curve as coined by Ebbinghaus,

which documents the rate of memory decay without further rehearsal.

3. Retrieval practice is the most effective method to improve our memories and thus learning, and it is exemplified by simple flashcards, which prompt for information in a vacuum without any other hints. There are numerous ways you can apply this in your daily life and numerous ways you can prompt for information.

Chapter 3. Active Learning Techniques

Researcher John Dunlosky and his associates conducted a thorough review of techniques and models related to learning in 2013. They examined 10 different methods, chosen because they were "relatively easy to use and hence could be adopted by many students." You'll probably recognize all of them as techniques that you've tried in the past with varying degrees of success.

Dunlosky's team rated each technique according to how well they were suited for the goal of learning and retention. As might be expected, the five models the team thought were *poor* for learning proved to be, arguably, the most commonly used and recognized:

Summarization. In this model, students are asked to write their own summaries of text to be learned. The point of summarization is to "identify the main points of a text and capture the gist of it while excluding unimportant or repetitive material." Dunlosky's team claimed summarization is a skill that only works if the student was already trained in how to do it. For the majority of students *without* that training, the technique couldn't be executed and wouldn't be effective. In other words, this might be effective, and in theory it is, but you are probably doing it wrong.

Highlighting. This long-standing, universally popular technique simply consists of marking pertinent text with a brightly colored ink marker or by underlining. The researchers found that highlighting might help a little if students were using it on an extraordinarily difficult text, but overall, they saw highlighting as a detraction from learning, as it doesn't help students draw additional meaning or inference from the study material.

Mnemonics. A practically ancient practice, mnemonics is the invocation of mental callbacks or shorthand—images, songs, phrases, or acronyms—to recall facts or information already learned—for example, using the phrase "Super Man Helps Every One" to identify the Great Lakes (Superior, Michigan, Huron, Erie, Ontario) or using pictures of objects in learning a foreign language. Researchers found that while it may help us quickly access memory of keywords, the potential of achieving "durable learning" from mnemonics was quite low. This might be connected to what we discussed with the relationship between rote memorization and concept learning.

Imagery use for text learning. A more abstract use of mental invocation than mnemonics, this device encourages students to conjure an image—mentally or on paper— to represent paragraphs or blocks of text they read. The researchers found this use of imagery "promising," although more study on the topic was needed. Overall, they found that the benefits of imagery use were limited to memory tests and text that already lent itself over to image creation or memory recall.

Rereading. Dunlosky's team found that although rereading and reviewing text was extremely common and easy to execute, it was only somewhat effective and mainly when rereadings of the text were spaced apart. They also maintained there wasn't compelling evidence that rereading had any effect on students' knowledge, abilities, or deep comprehension of the topic.

While these five techniques weren't without certain advantages—either their ease of use or their effectiveness when students knew how to use them *properly*—Dunlosky found their efficacy in retaining deep understanding, thoroughness, and applicability somewhat narrow and frequently subject to certain conditions. They held some value in superficial meaning or memorization, but far less in comprehension.

Technique	Utility
Elaborative interrogation	Moderate
Self-explanation	Moderate
Summarization	Low
Highlighting	Low
The keyword mnemonic	Low
Imagery use for text learning	Low
Rereading	Low
Practice testing	High
Distributed practice	High
Interleaved practice	Moderate

Above are the results of Dunlosky's study. Even though many methods have been debunked as ineffective, there was concrete evidence for the efficacy of other methods. Unsurprisingly, the difference between the two groups was the amount of active processing involved.

Five *Effective* Techniques

The other five strategies Dunlosky's team covered were deemed as the best for learning and retention:

- Practice testing

- Distributed practice

- Elaborative interrogation

- Self-explanation

- Interleaved practice

We've already discussed *practice testing,* otherwise known as retrieval practice, in Chapter 2. That's when you are looking at a blank piece of paper and are prompted to generate information without any further cues. *Distributed practice* is unique enough that it deserves its own set of guidelines, so we'll cover that method in the next chapter.

In this section, we'll discuss the remaining three techniques.

Elaborative Interrogation

If you've been around small children under age seven or so, you may have witnessed (or experienced, if you're a parent) a phenomenon we call "the why chain." This is when kids ask an initial question about the world—say, "Where does rain come from?"—and, after hearing our answer ("From clouds"), continue down a path of relentless questions to get at a definitive, ending answer ("Why don't the clouds hold in the rain?" "Why can't the clouds just fall to the earth still shaped like clouds?" "Why don't the clouds on a sunny day let rain go?").

Yes, this line of questioning can be a recipe for tedium. But it's reflective of a child's innate capacity for endless curiosity to get down to a final answer that brings their narrative to a satisfactory close. (For parents, of course, this point usually comes a lot earlier.)

Elaborative interrogation has something in common with that childlike inquiry, except it relates to more advanced topics that adults are (hopefully) liable to investigate. Simply put, elaborative interrogation is an effort to create explanations for *why* stated facts are true. Embody the mindset of Sherlock Holmes and seek to paint a thorough picture of what you wish to learn.

In elaborative interrogation, the learner creates questions as if working through a task. They inquire how and why certain objects work. Nothing is safe from this inquiry. They go through their study materials to determine the answers and try to find connections between all the ideas they're learning about. The answers the student gives form the basis of the notes they take.

"Why" questions are more significant than "what" questions, which primarily relate to the natures of identification and memorization. A line of "why" questions elicits a better understanding of the factors and reasons for a given subject. We can memorize all the parts of a flower—the petal, the stamen, the pistil, the receptacle, and so on—but the names alone mean nothing to us. We have to ask what each part of a flower does and why that role is integral to its lifespan.

This method is effective because it's simple and anyone can apply it easily. Elaborative interrogation does, however, require some existing knowledge about the topic to generate solid questions for yourself. Since you're reviving information you already had to clarify new concepts, this method might be best if you already have some experience with the subject of study.

Elaborative interrogation could proceed like this:

- Say you're studying the Great Depression of the 1930s. The first thing you'd ask would be, well, **what was it?** It was the biggest worldwide economic breakdown in the history of the industrialized world.

- **What caused the Great Depression?** A few key events, like the stock market crash of October 1929, the failure of over 9,000 banks, declines in consumer spending, high tax on imports from Europe, and drought conditions in the agricultural sector.

- Let's talk about the stock market crash. **Why did it happen?** Some experts were concerned about margin-selling, declines in the British stock market, out-of-control speculation, and some questionable business practices in the steel industry.

- ***Margin-selling? What was that? How did margin-selling work, and why was it a problem?*** Margin-selling (or margin-trading) is when an investor borrows money from a broker to buy stock. So many investors used it that most stock purchases were bought with this borrowed money. It worked so well that the stock prices went up—and when the asset bubble popped, prices fell off. Since the investor had no funds to repay the loan, both the broker and the investor had no profit to show for it.

And the chain of interrogation goes on from there. You use your study materials to obtain the answers to the "why" and "how" questions. Once you've sufficiently established those answers, you go back to the other aspects of the Great Depression and the stock market crash and determine how each aspect related to one another. *How did margin-selling affect the banks? How did margin-selling relate to the decline in consumer spending? Did the drought affect the trade issues with Europe?*

The range of topics for which you can use elaborative interrogation is practically limitless. For example, math students can use it to break down advanced calculations and establish patterns that might help in higher-level math topics. If you're studying human biology, you can use the technique to determine the specific conditions that lead to medical conditions like high cholesterol or heart arrhythmia. Even students of literature can use the technique to study motifs, trends, and themes in a particular author's work.

Self-Explanation

Self-explanation is thinking out loud. It involves explaining and recording *how* one solves or understands a problem as they work and establishes reasons for the choices made.

Like elaborative interrogation, self-explanation takes the form of a series of questions. But *these* questions are about how *you* plan on tackling the solution—not information from your study materials or your retained memory. For example, here's how self-explanation could progress:

- ***What is the problem?*** I need to put a playlist together for a wedding reception I'm DJ'ing.

- ***Okay, what do I usually put on a wedding playlist?*** Most of the songs are ones I play all the time, but there are other songs that the couple picks.

- ***So I have to ask them. Have I spoken to them about it yet?*** Not directly. We spoke a little bit about what *kind* of music they like, but they didn't mention any songs specifically. I might have to make a guess at a few of them.

- **What kind of music do they like?** They're into modern country music.

- **Have I played modern country at receptions in the past?** Yes, a few. But I don't follow country, so I'm not sure what songs to play.

- **How can I find out what modern country songs to play?** I could look up the latest charts online to see what country songs have been popular over the last few years.

- **Where do you get online charts?** Billboard is good. Wikipedia is fairly accurate when it comes to chart history.

We'll stop that line of questioning there because, honestly, this is far more work than a wedding DJ should do in this situation. But it shows the framework of self-explanation: you verbally state the problem, identify the issues, come up with possible solutions, analyze the effects of those solutions, and develop a final answer, result, or plan of action.

Self-explanation's most obvious trait is its simplicity. Most of us have internal monologues in some form or another throughout most of the day. Verbalizing these conversations in the context of problem-solving spurs more cognizant attention to how your mind works through a problem.

This method also allows you to gauge your true comprehension of a given subject. Properly carried out, self-explanation will prove whether you really understand a topic or have glossed over certain important concepts. It serves to monitor the process of your reasoning. It's also suitable for almost every conceivable subject, allowing you to see the gaps in your knowledge that need to be connected.

Self-explanation also encourages simplicity as a means to cement your understanding on a topic. If you feel your explanations are long, rambling, or protracted, you may not have grasped the subject as well as you may have thought.

For example, if you're over-explaining the subject of quantum mechanics by citing the in-depth details of past physicists' trials that support the study, try paring down the explanation to its barest core. From that point, you can start to do the same with more specific aspects of quantum theory.

The usefulness of self-explanation is especially helpful in scientific or technological topics, but it's adaptable for any subject. Literature students can use it to narrow down themes, historians can use it to explain events and historical patterns, and civics students can use it to understand living conditions or urban issues—there's really no restriction on how you can use it.

The Feynman technique, named for famous physicist Richard Feynman, is a specific application of self-explanation. It has four steps.

Step one: Choose your concept.

The Feynman technique is very widely applicable, so let's choose one we can use throughout this section: gravity. Suppose that we want to either understand the basics about gravity or explain it to someone else.

Step two: Write down an explanation of the concept in plain English.

Is this easy or difficult? This is the truly important step because it will show exactly what you do and do not understand about the concept of gravity. Explain it as simply, yet accurately, as you can in a way that someone who knows nothing about the concept would also understand.

Can you do it or will you resort to saying, "Well, you know . . . it's gravity!" This step allows you to see your blind spots and where your explanation starts to fall apart. If you can't perform this step, clearly you don't know as much about it as you thought, and you would be terrible at explaining it to someone else. You might be able to explain what happens to objects that are subject to gravity and what happens when there is zero gravity. But everything that happens in between might be something you assume you know but continually skip learning about.

Step three: Find your blind spots.

If you were unable to come up with a short description of gravity in the previous step, then it's clear you have large gaps in your knowledge. Research gravity and find a way to describe it in a simple way. You might come up with something like "The force that causes larger objects to attract smaller objects because of their weight and mass." Whatever you are unable to explain, this is a blind spot you must rectify.

Being able to analyze information and break it down in a simple way demonstrates knowledge and understanding. If you can't summarize it in one sentence, or at least in a brief and concise manner, you still have blind spots you need to learn about.

Step four: Use an analogy.

Finally, create an analogy for the concept. Making analogies between concepts requires an understanding of the main traits and characteristics of each. This step is to demonstrate whether or not you truly understand it on a deeper level and to make it easier to explain. You can look at it as the true test of your understanding and whether you still possess blind spots in your knowledge.

For example, gravity is like when you put your foot into a pool and the fallen leaves on the surface are attracted to it because it causes a barely seen impact. That impact is gravity.

This step also connects new information to old information and lets you piggyback off a working mental model to understand or explain in greater depth. The Feynman technique is a rapid way to discover what you know versus what you think you know, and it allows you to solidify your knowledge base.

Interleaved Practice

The final active learning method of this chapter represents a departure from what many might consider the established and logical way of learning a skill or a subject: devoting time to learning one subject in uninterrupted blocks, like eating all of your vegetables first before eating your dessert.

Blocking involves learning or practicing one skill at a time before progressing to another one. You don't move on from working on one skill until you've completed the routine—you finish Skill A before Skill B and finish Skill B before moving on to Skill C. Representing study time units as one letter, this practice would establish a pattern that looks like AAABBBCCC.

Interleaving disrupts that sequence. It mixes the practice of several related skills throughout the study session. So the pattern of interleaving would look like ABCABCABC.

For example, a beginning algebra student may be tasked with comprehending exponents, graphing, and radicals. Instead of taking each subject one at a time, they could start with exponents, break off and practice graphing, then work on the radicals of square roots, and then go back to studying exponents. When studying Shakespeare, one could divide portions of a study session switching between the playwright's comedies, tragedies, and historical plays. Taking it to another level, you could study Shakespeare, then mathematics, and then African history all in the same study block.

Interleaved practice at first might seem a haphazard, somewhat randomized way of learning in comparison—but which method actually works best? Research indicates that interleaving is actually much more effective for motor learning (physical movement) and cognitive (math) tasks.

Its advantage over block learning is surprising: tests indicated than interleaving produces a 43% increase in learning and retention over block learning.

Interleaving pushes a student out of the comfort zone of order and sequence. This disruption stands to make more of an impression on the student's mind than maintaining the study session's status quo. And it's also a form of retrieval practice: students regularly revisit recently acquired knowledge at a higher rate. The more often we can find information, call it back up, review it, and connect it with other subjects we already know, the more likely we are to understand and remember the information (Blaisman, 2017).

The blending of concepts or problems builds and reinforces stronger connections between them. Students generally perceive concepts as free-standing, self-contained bits of information with no apparent or obvious connections to other bits. Regularly reviewing material that's previously been covered facilitates discovery of these connections and encourages us to find unexpected bridges between different skills and ideas. Like retrieval practice, it brings our knowledge *out* of our banks of concepts and promotes active thinking about where they fit.

The benefits of interleaved practice are two-fold. First, it improves the brain's ability to discriminate between concepts. In blocking, once you know what the solution is, the hard part's over. With interleaving, each practice attempt varies from the last, so rote or automated responses don't work. Instead, your brain has to continually focus on finding different solutions. This process sharpens your ability to learn critical features of skills and concepts, which therefore helps you select the correct response and execute it.

Interleaving also strengthens memory associations. In blocking, you only need to hold one strategy in your short-term memory at a time. In interleaving, the strategy will always be different because the solution changes from one attempt to the next. Your brain is relentlessly engaged in calling forth different responses and bringing them into your short-term memory. Again, it's an active and more challenging approach—but it reinforces your neural connections among different tasks and responses, which enhances and improves learning.

The practice of interleaving can be effective in text-based learning as well, but a little more advanced preparation might be needed. The most important tip to remember is that interleaving isn't the same as multitasking, which you should avoid. Don't play *too* loosely with the disciplines you're learning—interleaving between chemistry, English lit, and ceramics is probably more trouble than it's worth, not to mention messy.

Rather, within a single study session, move between multiple topics. Try to set a limit on how many different angles or subjects you'll handle in a given study block—three is enough and four might be good for intense sessions—but once you're in, feel free to let your instincts guide you from topic to topic. Setting a timer for each topic is fine, but for some, the enforcement of an artificial limit might not be ideal for comprehension purposes.

Even if the subjects you interleaf don't vary too wildly, you still have some wiggle room. For example, you can juggle readings in English literature, European architecture, and Greek philosophy without too much shock to the system. Subjects that spur the finding of connections are especially helpful—blending studies in art theory, art technique, and the history of pop cultural art of the '60s could very well produce meaning that can easily be shared across all three concepts.

All the strategies we've detailed in this chapter take information we receive and turn it into a moving part. We don't just store it in our minds and move on to the next idea. Instead, we question the information, compare it, and use it to illuminate other information. By immediately putting new ideas to use and pulling out learned ideas to connect with the new ones, you're turning education into action that deepens its meaning. When that happens, it's something you'll have a hard time forgetting.

Takeaways to Accelerate Your Learning

1. Passive learning activities like summarization and simple highlighting have been proven as ineffective. If you want to learn, you must engage your mind in an active manner. This is more difficult, so understandably it is done less.

2. Elaborative interrogation is the process of explaining concepts to yourself and acting like Sherlock Holmes to understand what is involved in any concept. "Why" and "how" questions tend to work the best.

3. Self-explanation is the process of talking out loud to yourself to discover what you know and don't know. The Feynman technique is a special application of this technique where you are able to discover blind spots based on how well you can use self-explanation with any given concept.

4. Interleaved practice is the act of mixing up your subjects of study as opposed to learning subject by subject in segregated blocks. This works because you grow stronger associations and links to various information.

Chapter 4. Spaced Repetition; No Cramming

Spaced repetition—otherwise known as distributed practice—is just what it sounds like.

In order to commit more to memory and retain information better, space out your rehearsal and exposure to it over as long of a period as possible. In other words, you will remember something far better if you study it for one hour a day versus 20 hours in one weekend. This goes for just about everything you could possibly learn. Additional research has shown that seeing something 20 times in one day is far less effective than seeing something 10 times over the course of seven days. Unlike the approaches in the previous chapter, which capitalize on being more active, this approach capitalizes on how Ebbinghaus's forgetting curve works and battles it.

Spaced repetition makes more sense if you imagine your brain as a muscle. Muscles can't be exercised all the time and then put back to work with little to no recovery. Your brain needs time to make connections between concepts, create muscle memory, and generally become familiar with something. Sleep has been shown to be where neural connections are made, and it's not just mental. Synaptic connections are made in your brain and dendrites are stimulated.

If an athlete works out too hard in one session like you might be tempted to in studying, one of two things will happen. The athlete will either be too exhausted, and the latter half of the workout will have been useless, or the athlete will become injured. Rest and recovery are necessary to the task of learning, and sometimes effort isn't what's required.

Here's a look at what a schedule focused on spaced repetition might look like.

Monday at 10:00 a.m. Learn initial facts about Spanish history. You accumulate five pages of notes.

Monday at 8:00 p.m. Review notes about Spanish history, but don't just review passively. Make sure to try to recall the information from your own memory. Recalling is a much better way to process information than simply rereading and reviewing. This might only take 20 minutes.

Tuesday at 10:00 a.m. Try to recall the information without looking at your notes much. After you first try to actively recall as much as possible, go back through your notes to see what you missed, and make note of what you need to pay closer attention to. This will probably take only 15 minutes.

Tuesday at 8:00 p.m. Review notes. This will take 10 minutes.

Wednesday at 4:00 p.m. Try to independently recall the information again, and only look at your notes once you are done to see what else you have missed. This will take only 10 minutes. Make sure not to skip any steps.

Thursday at 6:00 p.m. Review notes. This will take 10 minutes.

Friday at 10:00 a.m. Active recall session. This will take 10 minutes.

Looking at this schedule, note that you are only studying an additional 75 minutes throughout the week but that you've managed to go through the entire lesson a whopping six additional times. Not only that, you've likely committed most of it to memory because you are using active recall instead of passively reviewing your notes.

You're ready for a test the next Monday. Actually, you're ready for a test by Friday afternoon. Spaced repetition gives your brain time to process concepts and make its own connections and leaps because of the repetition.

Think about what happens when you have repeated exposure to a concept. For the first couple of exposures, you may not see anything new. As you get more familiar with it and stop going through the motions, you begin to examine it on a deeper level and think about the context surrounding it. You begin to relate it to other concepts or information, and you generally make sense of it below surface level.

All of this, of course, is designed to push information from your short-term memory into your long-term memory. That's why cramming or studying at the last minute, isn't an effective means of learning. Very little tends to make it into long-term memory because of the lack of repetition and deeper analysis. At that point, it becomes rote memorization instead of the concept learning we discussed earlier, which is destined to fade far more quickly.

As an illustration of the applicability of spaced repetition, Paul Pimsleur discovered that for his audio-based language learning program, there were very specific pauses that led to increased learning. In other words, there were very specific intervals of time between the repetitions that showed better language learning and retention.

The intervals he discovered were 5 seconds, 25 seconds, 2 minutes, 10 minutes, 1 hour, 5 hours, 1 day, 5 days, 25 days, 4 months, and 2 years. This shows the importance of repetition, especially soon after initial exposure.

Learning is effectively created when they are processed and analyzed on a deeper level, because they form a vivid mental image versus a set of facts and descriptions that the brain filters as boring and useless.

When you set out to learn something, instead of measuring the number of hours you spend on something, try instead to measure the number of times you revisit the same information after the initial learning. Make it your goal to increase the frequency of reviewing, not necessarily the duration. Both matter, but the literature on spaced repetition or distributed practice makes clear that breathing room is necessary.

Cramming

Despite the warnings against cramming we have all read, many of us still won't heed them.

That's for good reason. We get busy with other things and can't break our stride to review something even for five minutes. We have many other subjects to learn and study. We just feel lazy and tired at the end of a long day. These are all legitimate—and, at the very least, realistic—excuses.

We know this isn't the most effective way to learn, but unfortunately, it's what we're stuck with sometimes. There's a saving grace— recall that most effective learning targets long-term memory. That's the main goal of spaced repetition: to make the leap from short-term memory to long-term memory, where you no longer have to rehearse or practice it to remember. You can simply recall it with a bit of thought, and it's in your brain for an indefinite period of time.

To cram for a test, exam, or other type of evaluation, we don't need material to make it to our long-term memory. We just need it to make it slightly past our working memory and be partially encoded into our long-term memory. We don't need to be able to recall anything the day after, so it's like we only need something to stick for a few hours.

You might not be able to do true spaced repetition if you are cramming at the last minute, but you can emulate it in a small way. Instead of studying subject X for three hours only at night, seek to study it one hour each three times a day with a few hours between each exposure.

Recall that memories need time to be encoded and stick in the brain. You are doing the best imitation of spaced repetition you can with what you have available. To get the most out of your limited studying time, study something, for example, as soon as you wake up, and then review it at noon, 4:00 p.m., and 9:00 p.m. The point is to review throughout the day and get as much repetition as possible. Remember to focus on frequency rather than duration.

During the course of your repetition, make sure to study your notes out of order in order to see them in different contexts and encode better. Also use active recall versus passive reading. Don't be afraid to even intersperse unrelated material in to reap the benefits of interleaved practice. Make sure to focus on the underlying concepts that govern the information you are learning so you can make estimated guesses about what you don't remember.

Make sure that you're reciting and rehearsing new information up to the last minute before your test. Your short-term memory can hold seven items on its best day, so you might just save yourself with a piece of information that was never going to fit into your long-term memory. It's like you're juggling. It's inevitable that you drop everything, but it could just so happen that you're juggling something you can use. Make use of all types of memory you can consciously use.

Flashcards are one of your best cramming aids. They force recall, and they aren't passive. You must actively recall and state what is on the other side of the flashcard, and it's this act of accessing a potential memory that cements its status.

In order to make best use of your flashcards, commit to making two sets. The first set will contain mere definitions and single concepts: one-word prompts for one-word or one-sentence answers.

The second set of flashcards will contain as much information about a single concept as possible so you will be forced to recall all of that with the prompt of a single word. This is also known as chunking information, where it's advantageous to your short-term memory (which can only hold on average seven items) to remember information as a large chunk rather than as smaller, individual components. This means that when you put more information on each flashcard, that set of information becomes one item versus five items.

When you go through your flashcards, put the cards you got wrong back into the middle or front of your stack so you see them sooner and more frequently. This helps you work through your mistakes and commit them to memory more quickly.

Overall, you are familiar with flashcards and have likely used them, so there isn't much for me to add here that would teach you something new. Just make sure to understand that flashcards aren't a passive activity. You need to actively recall the other side of the flashcard, recite it out loud, and then strive to recall more from that single prompt.

Finally, in processing raw information through rote memorization, use mnemonics as often as possible. A mnemonic device is most commonly seen as an acronym, where the first letter might represent a word for each. You can make mnemonics for just about anything.

For example, the colors of the rainbow are far more easily remembered as ROY G BIV (red, orange, yellow, green, blue, indigo, and violet).

Not much more clarification is necessary here other than to note that while acronyms are the most common, you can create phrases as mnemonics as well. The point is to give meaning to something that you can more easily remember, and this can be different for everyone. Here are a couple more examples.

The classification system for organisms is far more easily remembered as Devoted (or some other D-word) King Philip Came Over For Good Soup (domain, kingdom, phylum, class, order, family, genus, and species).

The order of the planets of our solar system can be My Very Easy Method: Just Say Understand Now (Mercury, Venus, Earth, Mars, Jupiter, Saturn, Uranus, and Neptune). The list goes on. The more vivid and outlandish the acronym or imagery, the better and easier to remember.

Takeaways to Accelerate Your Learning

1. Spaced repetition is the mother of effective learning, but sometimes that's impractical in daily life. Adjust your focus onto frequency over duration in general, and your learning will improve by leaps and bounds.
2. Cramming is sometimes unavoidable, but you can still implement spaced repetition into smaller periods of time. You can also

use interleaved practice and concept learning to speed up your learning.

3. Flashcards and mnemonics are helpful to learning as much as possible in a short period of time because they are effective at organizing information and breaking it into chunks.

Chapter 5. Make Learning Secondary

"That is the way to learn the most, that when you are doing something with such enjoyment that you don't notice that the time passes."—Albert Einstein to his son, Hans Einstein

There is a lot of wisdom to unpack in that simple sentence Einstein once uttered to his son, and it ties directly into the focus of this chapter.

It's a straightforward premise. If you are lucky enough to be consumed with a goal or objective, and achieving that goal or objective happens to require the acquisition of skills or knowledge, then you won't even notice. Your learning and expertise become second nature all in pursuit of that goal.

I want to briefly repeat a story I've told elsewhere. I had a very motivating goal of talking to a girl in my Spanish class, Jessica. She tended to turn around and ask me for help because she was perhaps the one person who paid less attention than me in class, so I vowed to get better at Spanish so she would continue talking to me.

In this pursuit for her attention, I studied Spanish like a madman and even researched obscure references and vocabulary to impress her. I didn't know it at the time, but I had made learning secondary, and the pursuit of my goal was my biggest priority. Every new word or phrase I learned was one I could use for another purpose.

I learned as a by-product, and that is perhaps the easiest way to learn.

Here's another example that involves my older sibling. When he was growing up, the Internet was just starting to become popular. Of course, with the Internet came chat rooms, message boards, and all sorts of communication with people that weren't right next to you. It opened the world up for many people. I remember watching him sit at the family computer and struggle to type.

One day he downloaded some sort of chat program, which I now realized was AOL Instant Messenger—the infamous AIM that nearly every adolescent, teenager, and young adult used at the time. It couldn't have been one or two weeks later that I walked past him at the computer again and couldn't help but notice how noisy and busy the keyboard was. His typing speed had probably quadrupled in just that week since downloading AIM. He became nearly obsessed with chatting online, and that obsession translated into competency quite quickly.

He had made learning how to type secondary in pursuit of his primary goal of talking to his friends online more quickly! All he wanted to do was type faster so he could tell jokes with proper timing and not get beat to the punch line by his friends, and he found a way to get that done through typing more quickly. His accuracy and so-called technique would probably have been better if he attended typing classes, but he was an incredibly fast typist, with all credit going to AIM.

Here's a final example to illustrate that making learning secondary can lead you to learning and knowledge without you even realizing it.

This story is about one of my friends from college. When he was still living in the dorms, he was surrounded by people who happened to play the guitar. They had all learned at some point when they were teenagers and brought their guitars to college to serenade women. Occasionally, they also lugged all of their guitars into the same room and jammed out to classic rock songs as a band.

Feeling left out, my friend asked if he could use one of their roommates' guitars when they weren't there. It wasn't a problem, so my friend began learning how to play guitar on his own, practicing the songs his dorm mates jammed to. It wasn't that he felt left out or wanted to fit in—he just saw music as a fun group activity and wanted to be able to participate.

The next time the group gathered to jam, he was able to join in on the fun, and when they went through various songs in their repertoire, he was able to learn on the fly and play quietly in the background before becoming more confident and playing more loudly. He started to bond with these guys and learned more and better guitar so the group could play more complex tunes and solos.

He is another shining example of why, if possible, you should make learning secondary. Think Daniel from *The Karate Kid*, who was forced to paint and clean and realized he was actually learning karate.

Given the proper motivation, you can make it so learning and knowledge isn't a chore and is rather a rung on the ladder to your overall goal and sense of gratification. What's more important when you have a bigger goal is that you focus on efficiently making something work. You might not be worried about the specifics as much, but you will probably have the same end result. From there, you have the choice to start deliberate practice, rehearsal, and fine-tuning everything, but simply having the right motivation will get you to a point of competency and even make you stand out. It's simply not as painful when you are chasing something greater versus learning for the sake or learning or being forced to.

Skill, expertise, and learning can all come as a by-product of your overall goal. What do we do with this knowledge?

Understand that a motivation other than learning and knowledge is your most powerful learning tool. You have to see the forest through the trees and understand the rewards and benefits of what your actions are leading toward. In essence, everything you learn or want to become better at is a tool on the way to your overarching goal or project.

Don't have a goal or project? Make one that will make the acquisition of a desired skill necessary but not the primary focus. For instance, if you want to learn better geography, start playing board games that require such knowledge. If you want to get better at skiing, start entering small, local competitions that will force you to improve. If you want to get better a typing, play a game that requires quick and accurate typing. If you want to learn a language more quickly, watch television shows that require greater vocabulary.

Make learning the journey, not the end point.

It's important to mention that it's not wise to always rely on motivation or inspiration. Those require you to be in a positive state of mind, which isn't always possible. It also puts you in a mindset where you have a prerequisite to learning and focusing. You need to feel inspired, you need to feel motivated, or you need to be in the right state of mind. This, we all know, definitely isn't always possible.

That's why I want to touch upon what I call the 10-minute rule. It works in two ways. First, if you don't feel like doing something, just do it for 10 minutes. Then you can stop. Of course, you'll rarely stop at the 10-minute mark because you'll have built up momentum and destroyed what was keeping you lazy: inertia.

Second, whenever you feel like stopping a task or quitting for the day, just give it 10 more minutes until you stop. You may not continue much past this, but giving yourself a specific deadline will make you want to finish as much as possible in that time, and it will make you just a tad bit more productive. Your motivation may be waning, but your discipline will keep you working.

The other big lesson of this chapter is that doing, using, and applying is, hands down, the most important part of learning. Recall the pyramid of learning where the most passive methods of learning yielded the least memory retention. When you apply your knowledge, you are at the participatory and active part of the pyramid. It's more work to be sure, and most of us like to slide down the path of least resistance.

Doing and getting your hands dirty allows you to find patterns and make connections that observation and study would never show you. I'd go so far as to say you will never master anything without some first-hand experience. Dan Coyle, talent researcher and scientist, suggested that the rule of two-thirds is most effective when learning or acquiring a new skill. You should spend one-third of the time reading and researching and the other two-thirds actually doing and practicing.

You can only learn so much about playing the guitar by watching videos and reading tutorials. Don't expect to be able to play like Jimi Hendrix the first time you pick the guitar up if you don't practice and do. If you're a complete neophyte, then you need to start with research and bone up on the ground rules and boundaries. Then you go and do.

Knowledge from research by itself is useless without the experience to back it up. When you combine those two, you gain intuition and judgment, which is usually the true goal.

Gamification

Another way to make learning relevant and motivating to you is the concept of *gamification*. Gamification is when you apply the principles that make games addictive to nongaming contexts. For instance, gamification in an office setting might be allowing people to "level up" if they work a certain number of hours or complete a certain number of milestones. This would serve to motivate people on two fronts: for the arbitrary level-up and to hit the actual work milestone.

Often, people have difficulty becoming motivated purely out of duty or obligation. That's where gamification is best used—if you can make someone focus on leveling up, you can motivate them to hit their work milestones as a by-product of wanting to level up. For instance, let's say that for each sale someone makes, they gain a point. If they accrue enough points, their title is upgraded from sales salmon, to sales tuna, to sales shark, to sales whale, to sales fisher. The idea behind gamification is to make people care about these levels and, in the process, make them care about their sales numbers.

You see this all the time with points, badges of honor, loyalty programs, and prizes for those who move up in the ranks. In reality, it's not about the points or badges at all—it's about motivating people to perform the underlying action that gets them the points or badges.

Gamification creates an extremely fertile ground for learning because it makes people forget about the unpleasant learning they are partaking in. Instead, it makes them focus on gaining points and gaining in general.

You can create the effect that you are actually being rewarded when you learn, as opposed to feeling annoyance and becoming burned out.

Let's take a famous example that has driven literally millions of dollars in revenue: the McDonald's Monopoly game. The McDonald's Monopoly game is a gamification strategy where customers receive stickers every time they purchase something at McDonald's. The stickers could be used in two ways. First, they could be used to complete a Monopoly board, and the more complete it was, the better chance you had for winning a prize. Second, certain stickers by themselves bestowed rewards and gifts like free hamburgers and drinks.

For many, it became an obsession to try to complete the Monopoly boards or get free prizes—all of which could be accomplished by simply spending more money at McDonald's. The outcome McDonald's desired was clearly to increase their revenue, and by making people focus on progressing in the Monopoly game, they distracted people from the fact that they were spending much more money on McDonald's than they would have otherwise. People could see and taste their progress in the game—visually through how complete their Monopoly boards appeared and through taste because they would literally get free food relatively frequently.

The free food was a short-term and immediate reward that kept people returning on a day-to-day basis, while the completion of the Monopoly board was a long-term reward that kept people returning on a yearly basis— it gave purpose to the entire venture. Having both rewards was critical, because together they addressed short-term boredom and long-term lack of positive reinforcement.

Because of the gamification strategy employed, people ignored the fact that they were essentially spending a lot at McDonald's for very little tangible reward—the reward was advancing in the game itself. In 2010, McDonald's increased its sales by 5.6% in the United States solely by using this strategy. It's similar to how games at a carnival can be so profitable. People will pay a sum to throw beanbags and knock down a pyramid of cans for a prize worth less than a dollar. But it's not about the value of the prize; it's about accomplishing the goal of knocking down the pyramid.

It's not about the pain of learning—it's about the game and your own progress. Everything else becomes secondary, but even though it's secondary, it will still occupy a fair amount of your mental bandwidth. That sweet feeling of advancement to the next level is a huge psychological reward. We anticipate it, then we feel it, and then we immediately seek more of it by striving to level up once more. It's addicting.

How can you gamify your learning and create short-term and long-term incentives? It's not necessarily giving yourself levels and badges, because that doesn't quite work in the same way when it's self-generated. This can vary from person to person, and it might be most effective to involve others. One of the best examples is something I've personally experienced in the form of a workout tracker.

Many CrossFit gyms use a mobile application called SugarWOD to record statistics and level of performance for each workout. Just the act of entering this information at the end of the workout is motivating. Further, it's a social platform that allows users to view and give feedback on the workouts of friends. There are even standardized levels of performance so you can compare your workouts with other people and see how you measure up. Finally, tracking upward progress is incredibly gratifying and motivating. Perhaps social pressure is good motivation to learn.

In an ideal world, learning by itself would be the reward that motivates us all. Isn't it a wonderful feeling to be enriched and knowledgeable in the ways of the world? Isn't it a shame that there have been so many books written in human history, and even if you devoted all of your free time to reading, you wouldn't put a dent into that number?

Well, then there wouldn't be the need for books like this one. Learning is most effective when you don't have to think about the act of learning.

Takeaways to Accelerate Your Learning

1. Learning by itself is not enough to motivate most people most of the time. That's perfectly natural. The task then becomes to find relevance, meaning, and motivation in an end goal where learning is part of the process. You can design tasks around what you have to learn to make learning secondary.
2. The concept of gamification is another way to make learning secondary, as the game mechanics and progress indicators become primary—for example, level-ups,

badges, rewards, etc. A powerful form of gamification comes in the form of competition and social pressure and comparison.

Chapter 6. Mistakes in Learning

Learning is a fluid activity. It's taking concepts that were unknown or nebulous to us in the past, finding a way to funnel them into our understanding, and incorporating them into our lives as need be. There are plenty of learning techniques, as we've seen, but no actual rules.

As such, there are some traps and inefficiencies that can come up when we're trying to learn. They can be reduced with some disciplined approaches and organization. In this chapter, we'll examine some of these pitfalls and what to do to correct them. Simply put, most of us are making mistakes in our attempts to learn and we don't even know it. You may have caught some errors now by virtue of learning some techniques presented thus far in this book, but that's just the beginning.

Fixed versus Growth: What's the Right Mindset?

Dr. Carol Dweck of Stanford University has studied attitudes toward learning for decades, as covered in her book *Mindset: The New Psychology of Success*. Dweck determined that most people adhere to one of two mindsets: fixed or growth.

People with the fixed mindset believe that talent and intelligence are inborn genetic traits. You either have talent or you don't. You were either born with intelligence or you weren't. There's nothing you can do that will change that fact, because it's just your fate. You can imagine how this might affect your efforts and attitudes toward learning new things.

Those with the growth mindset, on the other hand, believe that talent, intelligence, and capability can be developed as one grows. Through work, effort, and struggle, a person can *become* talented or intelligent. To the growth mindset, failure isn't fatal; it's just another step on the learning curve. If there is effort, there will be *some* change and improvement.

Dweck found that people with the fixed mindset tended to focus their endeavors on tasks with high chances of success, which came from the desire to "look smart." They steered away from jobs where any kind of struggle was involved. They avoided obstacles, ignored criticism, and felt threatened by others' successes. They also tended to not try new things or experiment because they felt failure was imminent.

People with the growth mindset, Dweck asserted, were more open and embraced challenges. They believed that tenacity and effort could change the outcome of their learning. They persisted through barriers, listened to critical feedback from others, and used other people's successes as inspiration and learning opportunities.

How you interpret challenges, setbacks, and criticism is your choice. You can interpret them through a fixed mindset and say you don't have the talent or ability to succeed, or you can use the growth mindset to use those obstacles as openings to stretch yourself, ramp up your strategic efforts, and expand your skills. You might be able to guess which is more conducive to accelerated learning and exposure to anything new—which one do you think is a mistake in learning?

Dweck's most revelatory research explored how these mindsets are created. Not surprisingly, it likely starts early in our lives. There's no intention here to skew to Sigmund Freud's perspective that everything we are was a result of our childhood experiences, but there are undoubtedly more connections than meet the eye.

In one seminal study, Dweck and her colleagues offered four-year-olds a choice:

they could either redo an easy jigsaw puzzle or try a harder one.

Children who showed fixed mentalities stayed on the safe side and chose the simpler puzzles that would affirm the abilities they already had, whereas the kids with growth mentalities considered the mere *option* strange: why would someone want to do the same puzzle over and over and not learn anything new?

The fixed-mindset children were focused on results that would guarantee success and give them the appearance of being smart. The growth-minded kids wanted to stretch their abilities. For them, the definition of success was *becoming* smarter. Ultimately, the growth-minded kids did what they wanted to do because they weren't necessarily concerned about possibilities or failure.

Dweck's study got even more interesting. She brought adults into the brainwave lab at Columbia University to study how their brains behaved as they answered questions and received feedback.

The fixed-mindset kids were only interested in feedback that reflected their present abilities. They turned a deaf ear to information that might have helped them learn and improve their performance. Strikingly, they showed no interest in hearing the right answer to a question they had gotten wrong—they had already labeled their answer as a failure and had no further use for it.

People with a growth mindset, though, paid keen attention to information that would help them gain knowledge and develop new skills. For them, there was no shame in getting the answer wrong, and the explanation of the right answer was welcomed as a great help in their development. The growth-mindset kids' priorities were learning—not the binary ego trap of success or failure. What manifests in childhood can stay with us for an entire lifetime if not addressed.

Fortunately, no matter how deeply a fixed mindset is ingrained in a person, it doesn't have to be a permanent condition as they might believe. Mindsets are malleable and can be taught. It turns out old dogs *can* learn new tricks.

Dweck and her colleagues developed a technique they called "growth mindset intervention." The usage of the word "intervention" might make it sound like a mid-scale invasion, but the beauty of the idea is how minor the adjustments really are. Small changes in communication—even in the most innocuous comments—can have long-lasting implications for a person's mindset.

One key area of focus in this technique is the nature of praise. Complimenting someone's process ("I really appreciate how you struggled with that problem") rather than their innate trait or talent ("You're so clever") is an easy but powerful way to promote the growth mindset.

Talent praise only reinforces the notion that success or failure rests on an inborn, unchangeable, static, and stagnant trait. Process praise applauds the effort and work— the *action* that's taken to get to the next step.

You want to reinforce the idea that talent is unimportant, whereas effort is everything.

You can predict how process praise might work in the classroom: "I know that chemistry lab had a couple of issues, but you worked right through them" or "I'm impressed with how thoroughly you worked on this term paper." But it's easy and effective to transmute that mindset in our everyday existences in the home and workplace: heighten the value of the process, maintain open channels of communication and constructive criticism, and build upon what we learn in the process for future projects. This is something you can do for others and also yourself in how you evaluate your actions and behavior in the face of learning.

The Myth of Tailoring Learning Styles

The notion of different learning styles has been a topic of conversation and endorsement in educational circles (not to mention publishers who sell teaching guides). Following close behind is the encouragement that teachers tailor their efforts to appeal to students more oriented toward a particular learning style over another. The theory says some students learn better when the material is presented visually, while others prefer verbally, logically, or some other manner. Of course, the same people who endorse these approaches just happen to be selling products that cater to each type of student. How convenient!

But does science exist that supports tailoring learning styles? In other words, are some people's brains just wired differently in this regard so that information ceases to become information if it isn't presented in the right style? Well, the learning styles in discussion are well known, and in an anecdotal way, they even make logical sense:

- Visual (spatial): Prefers learning through images, pictures, colors, and maps.

- Aural (auditory-musical): Leans toward learning through hearing sound and music.

- Verbal (linguistic): Chooses to use words, in both speech and writing—books, lectures, etc.

- Physical (kinesthetic): Prefers using the body, hands, and sense of touch. Typically enjoys sports and exercises.

- Logical (mathematical): Favors logic, reasoning, and systems, particularly finding patterns and connections between unrelated elements.

- Social (interpersonal): Likes to learn in group settings with open communication and exchange with others.

- Solitary (interpersonal): Tends to be more private and independent as well as self-reflective and personal.

It's not a stretch to say that some students consciously *like* some ways of learning over others. I certainly enjoy some activities better than others and, in doing so, may create a self-fulfilling prophecy for myself based on enjoyment. There are even some biological factors that appear to support the theory, as there are different brain structures for each of these types of functions that the learning style corresponds to:

- Visual: The occipital lobes at the back of the brain manage the visual sense. Both the occipital and parietal lobes manage spatial orientation.

- Aural: The temporal lobes handle aural content. The right temporal lobe is especially important for music.

- Verbal: The temporal and frontal lobes, especially two specialized regions called Broca's and Wernickeï's areas.

- Physical: The cerebellum and the motor cortex (at the back of the frontal lobe) handle much of our physical movement.

- Logical: The parietal lobes, especially the left side, drive our logical thinking.

- Social: The frontal and temporal lobes handle much of our social activities. The limbic system (not shown apart from the hippocampus) also influences both the social and solitary styles. The limbic system has a lot to do with emotions, moods and aggression.

- Solitary: The frontal and parietal lobes, and the limbic system, are also active with this style.

But?

There's no scientific evidence to suggest that the brain works in such fragmented ways. The only data produced to support the theory is presented by poorly run studies or misinterpretation of certain conclusions. The myth—or "neuromyth"—of learning styles is starting to meet more resistance lately, but there's still an adherence to the idea. In fact, there's plenty of evidence to suggest that all learning styles are equally effective when you account for attention and preference.

Paul Howard-Jones, a researcher at Bristol University, said that tailoring learning styles and other neuromyths are "misconception(s) generated by a misunderstanding, a misreading, or a misquoting of facts scientifically established by brain research to make a case for use of brain research in education or other contexts."

There's a risk in assuming that there's only one style that we should adhere to. We'd be doing a disservice to our range of ability and missing out on other potentially effective methods and mediums. Such an opinion tends to become a self-fulfilling prophecy that you'll only pay attention to one method and reject the others. That can only work to your detriment.

How do we handle this in our daily lives? There are certain things we gravitate toward based on our talents and preferences, but that doesn't mean others won't work. The best way is to mix mediums and strive to include multiple styles of learning.

The multiplicity of available media in our current landscape makes this an easier task to pull off than even just a few years ago. If you wanted to learn more about baseball, you could read an ample number of books, listen to audiobooks or even musical pieces about the sport, watch a movie about baseball (or the documentary series by Ken Burns), refer to applicable YouTube videos, and immerse yourself in the experience at an actual game, whether as a watcher or, if you can manage it, a player.

If you seek to learn in only one style, your options will be limited. Your options may even be terrible, whereas materials in other styles might be far superior. There is also the benefit of mixing and matching different types of media to gain full perspective of whatever you are trying to learn.

This same approach can be used in any subject that's got enough audio, visual, and textual content to use in learning. Frankly, there aren't many that don't. History, mathematics, foreign languages, music, and even practical arts like woodworking or computer skills all have various forms of media with valuable information. Incorporate it into your study plans as much as you like, and don't feel the need to chain yourself to a categorization that has no scientific basis, no matter how logical it may appear to be.

Taking Lazy Notes

Frequently, when a teacher delivers content, usually through a lecture, he or she gives students a handout that contains prewritten notes on the topic. This often takes the form of note pages that can be generated automatically from a PowerPoint presentation. The teacher may mean this to be a nice and convenient favor—but it's very bad for learning.

Learning happens when it's active and at least partially self-driven. When you're taking notes and organization information yourself, you're synthesizing it and making it personal. You're not digesting—poorly, usually—someone else's structure of teaching and engaging your own brain activity.

The information you get is presented in a linear fashion, but to make it meaningful, you might have to take a less predictable route. By writing notes in your own words—

somewhat similarly to retrieval practice—you must to think about the ideas in your text and coursework and how you can explain them in a coherent way. The simple act of taking active and fresh notes can be transformative.

Learning proper note-taking will help you retain, analyze, and finally remember and learn what you've read. You don't use what worked for someone else and try to force it down; instead, you create your own material and organize it in a manner that makes sense to you.

There are commonly said to be four main stages of effective and great notes:

- Note-taking
- Note editing
- Note analysis
- Note reflection

Most of us may not get past the second step—if we get there at all. But the latter three steps are where the magic happens because it's when you dive a level deeper than simple information retention. That's when you organize your own thoughts, analyze the connections, and reflect on how everything fits into the bigger picture. The most famous method of note-taking is called the *Cornell method*, and it actually encompasses much of the aforementioned four stages of great notes. Here's how it works.

On your handwritten sheet for note-taking (writing by hand is key), split it down the middle and into two columns. Label the right column "Notes" and label the left column "Cues." Leave a couple inches empty at the bottom of the page and label that section "Summary."

You now have three distinct sections, but you will only be taking notes in the Notes section. This is where you take normal notes on the bigger concepts with supporting detail as concisely as possible. Write everything you need to make a thorough assessment of what you're learning. Make sure to skip some space between points so you can fill in more detail and clarification at a later point. Draw charts and diagrams, make lists where appropriate, and give your best effort to capturing what matters. You don't need to think about organization or highlighting while you are taking the initial notes. Just write what you hear or read and give as complete of a picture as possible.

After you're done taking notes, move on to the left Cues side. This is where, for each section or concept, you filter and analyze the Notes side and write the important parts on the Cues side. Where the Notes side is more of a jumbled mess, the Cues side is a relatively organized account of the topic at hand— basically, the same information is on each side. Write the main supporting facts and anything that matters but in a more organized way. There is the added benefit of having to go through your notes immediately and synthesizing everything and drawing out what's important and what's not.

Finally, after you're done with the Notes and Cues sides, move to the Summary section at the bottom. This is where you attempt to summarize everything you've just taken notes on into a few top-level ideas and statements, with only the important supporting facts or exceptions to the rules. You want to say as much in as few words as possible because, when you review your notes, you want to be able to understand quickly and not have to deconstruct and analyze all over again. You want to be able to skim the Summary and Cues section and move on.

There are similarities between the Cornell method and the four stages of note-taking, but in each case, you have created your own study guide. Better yet, you also have the entire process you used to create it documented on the same page, from original notes to synthesis and summarization. You have a record of information that allows you to go as deep as you want or refer to whatever you want. The most important part is that you've created something that has personal significance to you because you've phrased everything in a way in which you derive meaning. You are making the information fit your mental scheme, not the other way around.

Overall, taking notes is not a lazy, passive activity. That's the real secret of great notes. They are intended to serve as something you can refer to, instantly understand, and find helpful, as opposed to having to decipher them. This won't work if you have to first try to understand someone else's sense of structure and organization.

Peter Brown, author of the book *Make It Stick*, simplifies this point on notes: he maintains that when no effort is put into the learning process, it doesn't last very long. What exactly does this mean?

In one study Brown cited, students were allowed to copy notes word for word on some material but were asked to rephrase *other* material in their own words. When these students were tested later, they did a far better job of recalling the material they had paraphrased themselves.

It may be convenient—for the students, if not the professor—to provide written notes for lectures. But the lack of effort this arrangement inherently has will handicap the student. In fact, the less effort and involvement a student is able to use, the worse the learning will be.

Plan your note-taking style in advance and bring everything you need to the lecture. Different colored pens, highlighters, Post-it notes, multiple binders—whatever implements that you've designed that help *you* learn. Try to keep your notes as concise as possible, with abbreviations, legends, or acronyms, and write down only the information that matters (though you get to decide what that is).

How can we make these note-taking principles relevant to the rest of our lives? In other words, how can we make sure we are paraphrasing everything we want to learn for ourselves? How can we ensure we expend effort and make learning as active as possible in the real world?

This is where the problem-solving we developed in school environments becomes real. But it's also representative of the truism that learning doesn't stop when we're out of school—actually, our state of learning won't die until *we* do.

We can't say enough about the benefits of personal documentation, whether it's for everyday functionality, work issues, interpersonal relationships, or just self-expression. Taking notes on anything we go through or experience on a daily basis and creating an organized system to make these notes accessible later helps us retain knowledge we'll need in future practical applications.

Whether taken by hand (which we still enthusiastically endorse) or by digital applications (which we'd be foolish to declaim), structuring the events of your life—raising a family, starting a business, pursuing a hobby—into a narrative, through your own words and notes, is an almost fail-safe way to derive continued meaning and personal value from your life.

Learning is defined by trial and error. Making a mistake in learning is almost never a fatal derailment from our path through education. Like all of the solutions we present in this book, these mistakes are solved by practice and adjustments in our mental approach. If you address mistakes the same way we suggest you do with the topics you study—actively, not passively—then these errors will be fewer and further between.

Takeaways to Accelerate Your Learning

1. What kind of mindset do you hold toward learning? Do you have a fixed mindset, or do you have a growth mindset? You want to ensure you have a growth mindset because that is the simple belief that you can learn and can improve. Check your internal monologue and change your language to change your mindset.

2. Don't fall into the myth that learning styles actually make a difference. They may

appear logical, but information is information. Don't sell yourself short and miss out on information presented through various media.

3. When you attempt to learn anything, you are trying to integrate it into your brain's organizational structures and methods. To do this, you must learn how to take great notes to help yourself, and the Cornell method is perfect for that. On a more general note, the more effort you put into learning something, the greater staying power it will have.

Chapter 7. Building Expertise

After the floodgates of learning have been opened for a while, certain subjects or fields will pop up as areas in which we'd like to become fluent. As with our initial learning experiences, there are several theories, methods, and philosophies that lead us through the path of building expertise. It's important to find one that works for you.

This chapter offers a general overview of what's necessary to establish expertise in any field. Despite what others might tell you, there are indeed tried and true paths to become world-class at something—or at least far above average. It doesn't require innate talent—only a strategic and intelligent approach.

The 10,000 Hour Rule

In 1993, scientist Anders Ericsson made note of a group of Berlin psychologists who were researching violin players. They found that elite performers had averaged more than 10,000 hours of practice each. Players that weren't quite as accomplished only managed 4,000 hours each. This led Ericsson to theorize that world-class performance was directly correlated with a certain threshold of practice and rehearsal.

Author Malcolm Gladwell spread the word about the 10,000 hour rule in his book *Outliers*. Gladwell famously cited Bill Gates and the Beatles as examples of people who earned their mastery by amassing at least 10,000 hours of diligent practice before they broke through as experts. Thus, it was dubbed the 10,000 hour rule.

The old joke— "How do you get to Carnegie Hall? Practice!"—rings true here. The 10,000 hour rule suggests the key to becoming a world-class expert is just a matter of grinding over time. The maxim also strengthens our assertion that talent or intelligence aren't what propel people to success.

The 10,000 hour rule can apply to virtually any aspect of our lives we want to master. Whether it's something that fits into our daily schedule like cooking or accountancy or a skill we want to pursue like gardening or computer programming, blocking out as much time as possible for purposeful exercise is a great start.

What does the 10,000 hour rule mean for us when we want to learn? Proficiency is a function of time and patience. None of the leaders we might model ourselves after got there by focusing on instant gratification—so temper your expectations, put in the time you need, and be patient with your progress.

It should be noted that the 10,000 hour rule has come under scrutiny by a few players in the research field. A study at Princeton University found that extensive practice only accounted for a 12% improvement overall—a respectable increase, but perhaps not the amount that crosses the line between novice to expert. The study also found that certain disciplines benefitted from intensive practice more than others: gaming, sports, and music were areas that reflected fairly high improvement under the 10,000 hour rule, whereas education and professional pursuits showed little or no improvement.

These newer findings indicate that there's something more to being an expert than just putting in the time required and nurturing talent—we also have to make practicing more focused and meaningful. Expertise *can* follow a certain number of hours spent if the hours were used in a smart way. Therefore, the 10,000 hour rule is not necessarily accurate.

Deliberate Practice

If 10,000 hours are spent in *deliberate practice*, then expertise will usually follow.

Deliberate practice is purposeful and systematic. Regular practice might entail unconscious repetition and rote chores, but deliberate practice requires focused attention with the specific goal of improving performance rather than just going through the motions. This is because the natural tendency of the human brain is to transform repeated behaviors into automatic habits.

For example, when you first learned to tie your shoes, you had to think very carefully about each step of the process. The more we repeat a task, the more natural it becomes until we can process the sequence of operations automatically.

To make deliberate practice work, then, you break a given task down into smaller components, drill through them repeatedly, and note what parts of the procedure you need to improve for better overall outcomes.

Putting deliberate practice to work in learning is not hard—just highly detailed. Computer science professor Cal Newport described how he mastered discrete mathematics. This branch of math study, *very* briefly stated, involves finding proofs for theories. Newport explained how he bought reams of white paper and then copied each "proposition" the professor would present at the top of each class session.

On his own, away from the classroom, Newport worked on the proofs. When he came to a concept he didn't understand, he consulted textbooks and online sources, in his own words, "to see if I could make sense of what I was writing down." Usually the process secured Newport's understanding of the problem; if it didn't, Newport consulted with his professor for feedback.

Near the end of the course, Newport had accumulated a massive stack of handwritten proofs. He "aggressively reviewed" them. He classified his proofs into ones that he could recall with little effort and those he needed to drill down. He continued to study the problematic ones—repetitively, exhaustively—until he finally extracted the last bit of understanding from them. After his final exam, Newport was told he'd achieved the highest grade in the entire class—not just on the final, but the whole course.

This is deliberate practice in action: setting up what you need, identifying the problem, repetitively examining it, testing yourself, getting feedback on your trouble spots, and focusing intensely until you're comfortable about your understanding. When you identify your overall goal as improved performance, it becomes clear on how to practice to build expertise. You are only as strong as your weakest link here.

Everything can be mastered using this intensive technique: the meaning of ancient texts, composition in music, themes in literature, operations in science, demographics in social studies, critiques in philosophy or theology—there's really no prohibition on what you can learn through deliberate practice.

There are some risks in this kind of exercise. The enemy of deliberate practice is mindless activity, and the danger of practicing the same thing over and over is that we'll *assume* we're making progress merely because we're gaining experience. But in truth, all we're doing is reinforcing our current *bad* habits— we're not improving or changing them.

Just do it. That's why we have to keep in mind that we must *do*. Learning and practicing something new might appear to be synonymous, but they actually produce profoundly different results. Passive learning isn't practice—just because you gain new knowledge doesn't mean you're learning how to apply it.

Active practice, on the other hand, is one of the greatest forms of learning. Practice is the only way your knowledge translates into meaningful contributions, and the mistakes you make along the way reveal new and important insights.

Watching an online business course or reading about a disaster in a developing nation will give you knowledge, but it's unproductive unless you actually follow through and start your business or donate to those in need. Learning can be valuable to you—but if you want to be valuable to others, you have to execute upon that knowledge in a significant way.

Measure yourself. Deliberate practicing involves keeping some kind of quantitative record of how you're doing. The first effective system of feedback on a task is measurement—what we measure is what we improve. Whether it's how many pages we're reading, how many push-ups we're doing, how many sales calls we're making, or how many words we're typing per minute, it's important to measure how we're doing. Measurement offers the only proof of whether we're getting better or worse.

Get feedback. It's almost impossible to perform a task and measure your progress at the same time. A good coach can track your progress, find small ways to improve, and hold you accountable for delivering your very best effort.

It's easy to see how feedback works in sports-related fields. One of the roles of a coach in football or basketball is to provide specific pointers on what an athlete needs to do to improve, even in the most minute detail. This structure works in learning environments, too. A math tutor can provide detailed feedback on the flow of your calculations and introduce some ways to streamline or improve the work you show.

Even in our daily lives, we have ample opportunity to receive feedback in almost any endeavor we work on. There are online help forums for every subject you can think up, from coding to cooking to car repair. Online classes from companies like Coursera and Udemy frequently give students ways to directly contact course instructors for help and direction on your projects. In any online community for an interest or hobby, you'll find several members who are more than happy to exchange information with you, including objective feedback on how you can improve your efforts.

The Dreyfus Model of Skill Acquisition

How can you tell if your learning has been effective and you've made the leap from neophyte to expert? Stuart and Hubert Dreyfus provided a model that can help you identify what stage you're currently at and what you need to do to advance to the next level.

In 1980, the Dreyfus brothers proposed a model in an 18-page report on their research at the University of California at Berkeley. Their report became highly influential in the field of learning and is still considered a potent roadmap in evaluating stages of knowledge.

The Dreyfus model states that a student passes through five distinct stages.

Novice. This is, of course, the starting point. The student is a blank slate who (in principle) knows nothing about the subject they're going to learn. In this stage the student gets to know the properties, objects, and especially the rules they'll need to follow. They should spend the vast majority of their time learning the rules of conventions.

Advanced beginner. The student has gotten the basic rules down at this point. Now they take their knowledge as learned in classroom confines and start applying it to real-world situations. They'll still make mistakes, but they're making headway. They should spend equal times practicing as learning the rules and conventions.

Competence. At this point, the student understands all the rules of the skill they're developing to the extent that they have to be selective about which rules they can use and which to ignore. It can be confusing, and they'll still make a lot of errors, but they'll be more aware of and learn from them. At this point, they should spend most of their time practicing instead of learning the rules and conventions.

Proficiency. Now the student is fluent and very conscious about their performance. They know it well enough to be able to reliably choose what approaches to take. The student still listens and observes others for ideas— and still must practice heavily to move up to the next level—but they're sure of themselves and their path. At this point, their knowledge acquisition phase should be over and they should be practicing to improve and create unconscious habits.

Expert. The student now becomes the master. They know immediately how to execute their skill with no need to analyze or think about it. The expert's performance looks seamless and a little magical—but it's actually the result of strong efforts at every stage. At this point, practice should only be to maintain skills that are largely unconscious and effortless.

The Dreyfus Model in Daily Life

Cognizance of the Dreyfus model makes it easy to apply the scheme to aspects of our everyday existence in service of becoming the experts we want to be.

Litemind.com suggests "[making] skills acquisition as productive as possible. By having a better idea of your skill level, you're able to give yourself exactly what's needed at that particular level. If you want novices to operate at their best, they will need unambiguous rules. On the other hand, bothering the experts with intricate rules and policies is a recipe for frustration and bringing their performance down because they are able to bend the rules and transcend them." For us, this means knowing what we can handle at any given stage in our learning, pushing toward the next only when we intuit that we're ready to learn the next phase.

To put it in terms of cooking, if you've finally mastered the art of boiling pasta, maybe it's time for you to move on from spaghetti sauce in a jar and make it from scratch. But you're probably not ready for something more complicated, like a flambé. On the other end, a master chef probably hasn't boiled dried pasta in decades and can flambé something without much thought whenever he feels like it. Map your progress to remember what skills match your level and whether you're ready to advance.

In the middling stages, feel free to *experiment with new techniques*. After you've established a rough competency in the novice stages, you can try different combinations or methods to determine what works. Can you use certain shortcuts in preparing your tax returns? Can you use water-based paint instead of oil-based in this portrait? Or to go back to the ever-popular food allegory, can you use crushed fennel seeds in this sauce recipe instead of sugar? This is the stage where failure's a learning tool, where technically there are no such things as mistakes. Take advantage of this stage (and enjoy it while you can).

As with almost all of our advice, *actively seek outside input or feedback* from people you trust—preferably ones who are open with their time and might have advanced to a higher level than you only recently. Many of them still remember what it was like to be in your shoes and, if they're not in some kind of competitive mode with you, would be happy to give you pointers on what you're doing. Keep in mind that the highest-level experts are probably not accessible, though—although a Food Network chef can tell you how to boil an egg, chances are they're not available for feedback on that novice task. But many lesser-known lights closer to your stage are easy to find.

Overall, the Dreyfus model is reminiscent of *the four stages of competency,* which is another method of describing skill and knowledge acquisition. The four stages of competence are as follows:

- Unconscious incompetence: "I have no idea what I am doing wrong."

- Conscious incompetence: "I know what I am doing wrong, but I'm not good enough to stop it."

- Conscious competence: "I'm fine if I can focus and concentrate and rehearse all day."

- Unconscious competence: "I can wing it and even improvise without thinking about it."

The Pareto Principle: the 80/20 Rule

At the turn of the 20th century, Italian economist Vilfredo Pareto created a mathematical formula to describe the unequal distribution of wealth in his home country. Pareto observed that roughly 20% of Italy's population controlled 80% of the wealth.

In current times, that ratio is even wider apart, not to mention the source of hot debate. However, for our purposes, let's extract the 80/20 ratio without prejudice and apply it to other scenarios: the 80/20 rule states that in any set of things (workers, customers, etc.), a few—20%—are vital and the remaining 80% are considered trivial.

The value of the Pareto principle in management is to remind us to stay focused on the 20% that matters. Of all the tasks we perform throughout the day, one could say that only 20% of them actually matter. The tasks in that 20%, quite likely, will produce 80% of our results.

It's therefore critical that we identify and focus on that smaller group of functions and tasks. In fact, it applies to virtually all aspects of life:

- Business: 80% of sales come from 20% of all customers.

- Employee efficiency: 80% of results come from 20% of all employees.

- Happiness: 80% of happiness comes from 20% of relationships.

- Travel experiences: 80% of our travels can be summed up by highlights from 20% of our experience.

This ratio can help you focus on what makes a difference—what drives the great majority of your success or happiness—and avoid the diminishing returns of things you can improve that won't affect the bottom line much. Expertise comes because you excel at what matters, and in most cases, that's going to be only 20% of what's available for you to learn. Everything else shouldn't necessarily be ignored, but it should be downgraded in terms of priority so you can attack what really affects your bottom line. Learn the 20%

underlying actions or habits that experts have first and then see what's necessary.

For example, language expert Gabriel Wyner says that when you're beginning to learn a new language, focus only on the 1,000 or so most common words in that language first: "After 1,000 words, you'll know 70% of the words in any average text, and 2,000 words provide you with 80% text coverage."

Wyner explains the imbalance even further. Let's say you knew only 10 English words: "the," "(to) be," "of," "and," "a," "to," "in," "he," "have," and "it." If that was the extent of your vocabulary, how much of any text would you recognize?

According to Dr. Paul Nation, the answer is 23.7%. Those 10 words represent 0.00004% of the English language, which has over 250,000 words. But we use those 10 so often that they regularly make up nearly 25% of every sentence we write.

Let's say we eventually increase our vocabulary to a whopping 100 words—

including "year," "(to) see," "(to) give," "then," "most," "great," "(to) think," and "there." With that number, Dr. Nation says, we'd have the ability to understand 49% of every sentence uttered.

Let that sink in a bit—with only 100 words, we can recognize nearly half the content of every sentence. Let's be generous and fluff his numbers—that would still mean that with 200 words, we could recognize 40% of the content in each sentence. The fact that *less than one ten-thousandth* of all English words make of almost half of every sentence is kind of a big deal. That is a staggering demonstration of the Pareto principle.

Dr. Alexander Arguelles, another polyglot working in linguistics at the Regional Language Centre of the South East Asian Ministers of Education Organization, breaks it down even further. Arguelles says that every day, the number of words every single speaker of a given language uses is 750. Furthermore, only 2,500 words are needed for you to express anything you could possibly want to say. (Although some expressions might be a little awkward or strange, 2,500 words are technically all you need.)

That's the Pareto principle in an almost perfect nutshell. To extend it to our lives, take any subject you want to learn and break it down to the tasks that experts in the field have that matter—and those that don't.

In football, coaches use the 80/20 rule to determine which minority of the plays they call create most of the results. When they identify which 20% of those plays are most crucial to most of their team's struggles, they work a little bit harder on those specific plays to improve execution and, hopefully, results.

Let's take software development. Microsoft once determined that 80% of all bugs are in only 20% of the code of any given program or execution. (Even more starkly, 90% of all downtime comes from just 10% or less of all defects.) Locating and fixing the 20% most killer bugs is, therefore, a primary concern. It won't fix everything, but it'll fix enough to take care of the most pressing issues.

It's easy enough to take the Pareto principle into our everyday lives. What 20% of our spice rack is used in 80% of our dishes? What 20% of our online destinations make for 80% of our web usage? What 20% of our household budget covers the bulk of our monthly expenses?

Of course, the Pareto principle isn't a hard and fast doctrine for 100% of our lives. (Maybe not even 80%!) But it gives us a very reliable guideline about how a very small range of actions has such an outsized impact on how we live. When you're seeking to learn or improve the overall quality of your life, start on the smaller segments that have the most impact.

Being an expert requires a lifetime of learning and protracted effort. Yet at the same time, experts have to concede that they'll never *stop* learning, no matter how widely known they are for their expertise. The principles in this chapter set you up to be a discriminating and astute master who'll continually evolve, renew, and persist.

Takeaways to Accelerate Your Learning

1. Expertise is a natural consequence of learning. Ericsson stated that you simply need 10,000 hours of practice, but this wasn't quite accurate. You actually need hours of deliberate practice, which is when your only goal is to improve performance. This fundamentally changes how you rehearse because you are only as strong as your weakest link.

2. The Dreyfus model of skill acquisition documents how we gain expertise and what we tend to do at each of the five stages along the way. Similarly, the four stages of competency model describes how we feel about our behaviors and habits on the road to expertise. When you can identify where you are in each of these models, you'll know what you need to do next.

3. The Pareto principle is otherwise known as the 80/20 rule because in just about every walk of life, 20% of what the input will produce 80% of the output. This is easily

seen in language acquisition, where knowing 100 words has been said to impart the power to recognize 50% of most sentences.

Chapter 8. Teaching to Learn

There is unexpected value in observing how others synthesize information.

First, you will see how someone else learns and absorbs information. Sometimes you can visibly see someone's face light up when they *get it*, and this is no small feat in the process of learning.

Second, you will see how the act of teaching improves the learning of the teacher. In observing how people synthesize information, you can improve upon how *you* do it. Understanding both sides of the coin is a helpful exercise. This, of course, is the process of teaching others to help you learn. This chapter is about how learning to effectively teach others is a great method of learning in itself—and a good skill to have in general.

The Learning Pyramid

The infamous learning pyramid—also called "the cone of experience"—sheds light on why being able to teach is vital. In fact, much of what we talk about dances around the spectrum of more passive learning to be less useful and more active learning to be more impactful. This is what the learning pyramid encompasses.

Some may take it as gospel, but the numbers are best if they are seen as rough guidelines. However, they still showcase the differences of what we should strive for in our learning activities:

- 90% of what they learn when they teach someone else or use their skills immediately

- 75% of what they learn when they practice what they learned

- 50% of what they learn when engaged in a group discussion

- 30% of what they learn when they see a demonstration

- 20% of what they learn from audio-visual

- 10% of what they've learned from reading

- 5% of what they've learned from a lecture

These numbers aren't exact or necessarily even proven. As with most modern theories or modules of education, the learning pyramid faces its share of dissenters. However, it *does* show a general trend that's true: the more involved you are, the better you learn.

Without a doubt, teaching is one of the most involved, participatory, and non-passive types of interactions with new information we can have. Like self-explanation and the Feynman technique, teaching someone not only roots information in your mind; it forces you to see what you truly can explain and what you can't. Teaching yourself is good; teaching others is even better.

Teaching exposes the gaps in your knowledge. Having to instruct and explain doesn't let you hide behind generalizations: "Yeah, I know all about how that works. I'll skip it for now." That won't fly if you're explaining a process to someone else—you have to know how every step works and how each step relates to each other. You'll also be forced to answer questions about the information you're teaching.

Having to explain what's going on is essentially a test of your knowledge, and you either know it or you don't. If you can't explain to someone how to replicate something you are teaching, then you actually don't know it.

Let's take photography as an example. According to the learning pyramid, reading and lecturing combined take up 15% of your retained knowledge, which makes sense:

there's only so much you can learn about photography from a textbook or a lectern. Audio-visual aids and seeing demonstrations—what certain angles look like, how to use computers to filter a print—are yet more helpful in learning to take and process certain pictures. A group discussion about photography would unlock some memorable ideas, and of course, spending the time to practice taking and developing pictures makes solid impressions on your experience.

Now let's examine the bottom (or top, depending on your view) part of the pyramid related to teaching others. You're reinforcing the basic knowledge in others and explaining the principles, types, and general guidelines of photography. Theoretically, you're overseeing all the upper (or lower) segments of the pyramid for students and using your knowledge of the photography process as a guidepost for all of them. And this doesn't even include the pre-instruction time when you're preparing for your own class.

All those teaching activities are active agents that call upon what you already know—and remember when we said you get more from pulling something *out* of your brain than putting stuff *into* it? That's exactly what's happening with that 90% tier of the pyramid. You're actively extracting from your previously learned knowledge, sending it out, and reshaping it for others to understand and learn. In turn, that reinforces what you know and maybe deepens your experience a little in the process.

It's common that you even surprise yourself and find additional insights by explaining and reasoning out loud in a way that simplifies and condenses. Teaching forces you to create bite-sized chunks and teach replication—a task you may find far different than explaining theories or concepts.

The Protégé Effect

"Teaching to learn" isn't a radical or even particularly novel concept. In the field of education, it's already regarded as one of the best ways to learn. But there's another element to why teaching can be so helpful to the teacher.

Recent studies have given rise to something researchers call the "protégé effect." This process demonstrates that people who teach others work harder to understand, recall, and apply material more accurately and effectively. Tutors in general therefore score more highly on tests than their non-tutoring counterparts. Why do you think this might be?

To increase the usefulness of this effect, scientists have developed virtual pupils for students to tutor. These virtual students are known as "teachable agents" (TAs). Researchers at Stanford University, which is sort of a hotbed for this kind of technology, explain TAs as follows:

"Students teach their agent by creating a concept map that serves as the agent's 'brain.' An artificial intelligence engine enables the agent to interactively answer questions posed to it by traversing the links and nodes in its map. As the agent reasons, it also animates the path it is following, thereby providing feedback, as well as a visible model of thinking for the students. Students can then use the feedback to revise their agent's knowledge (and consequently, their own)."

Students working with a teachable agent are therefore on the opposite side of where they usually are in the typical teaching paradigm—instead of being the student, they're the teacher. The TAs serve as student models, and like all active students, they can ask questions and even give wrong answers. Trials have shown that students using TAs significantly outperform their peers who have only been studying for themselves, without TAs to serve as feedback.

Stanford scientists studied the effects of TAs on eighth-grade biology students. Some students were asked to learn biological concepts so they could teach their TAs. The rest were asked to develop an online concept map to demonstrate how their understanding of the concepts was organized. Results showed the students who worked with TAs spent more time engaged with the concept and displayed more motivation to learn. Simply put, the students put forth greater effort to learn for "teaching" their TAs than they did for themselves. They felt responsibility and accountability beyond themselves, and this made them put in the extra effort regarding their expertise—the protégés are depending on you!

The scientists at Stanford attributed three factors that spoke to the power of the protégé effect:

The ego-protective buffer. This is a sort of psychological shield that allows students to examine failure without the negative feelings it typically produces. This can be a powerful metacognitive force since students are more apt to reflect upon their learning without the emotional sting of disappointment.

Incrementalist view of intelligence. When the learning process is directed externally to support another's learning, students spend more time examining their own understandings. This helps students see how reviewing and revising their insight can impact their own learning.

Sense of responsibility. Teaching another person—or, in this example, the virtual TAs—motivates students to take more command over their own learning process. When they realize that what they say will be absorbed by another thinking unit, they're more meticulous about getting the information right to begin with.

Not all of us who aren't teachers or tutors have the opportunity to share our knowledge directly with willing students. However, thanks again to the miracle of technology, you can find plenty of online sites with message boards or forums, all filled with questions you can answer (or at least *find* the answers for). A nice site to start with—despite its somewhat unruly nature—is Quora.com, where users just literally ask questions of the hive-mind of the Internet. Many questions are very general, and some serve as bait for trolls or fanatics. But they're easily funneled out, and you're left with a lot of genuine inquiries asking for serious answers. It's a good, almost comically quick way to share information with others—more importantly, it allows you to reap the rewards of the protégé effect and learn better.

Strategic Questions

We sometimes forget that teaching is for the student, not for ourselves. In this relationship, the teacher rarely asks questions to elicit information about whom they're teaching. But by learning more about the student, we sharpen our focus on what we need to convey and what's missing from our own information. Different students have different experiences and gaps in knowledge, and each new angle can bring a different perspective for the teacher.

Questions give you a mirror to discover what you know and what you don't. They set up a comparison between other people's perceptions versus your own—except, in a sense, your perceptions are wrong, and those of others are right. Such questioning, therefore, serves as a method of self-correction.

Michael Bungay Stainer's book *The Coaching Habit: Say Less, Ask More & Change the Way You Lead Forever*, identified seven kinds of questions that arise in the environment of professional coaching and teaching. We can extract these seven questions and use them from a teaching standpoint to discover the stumbling blocks in learning, how we would overcome them, and how to explain to someone else how to overcome them:

What's on your mind? This is the "kickstart." It's a forward invitation to the student that encourages him or her to address the fact that there's some sort of problem, situation, or question they want to resolve. The student also sets the agenda with their answer to this question, which gives them a sense of controlling the discourse to some extent. That's empowerment for them: a safe place to start. If there are any prominent issues, here's where they will come out.

And what else? Stainer says this is his favorite of the seven questions. The response to the first question is almost always a summary view that describes the framework of the student's concern—but this question gets to something deeper about the problem that the student probably really wants to discuss. The student may focus more on a specific part of his first answer—or possibly realize that there's something else altogether that they're really worried about. Just think about how you answer people who ask how your day was. First, you inevitably say it was fine— nothing out of the ordinary. Then you say what's really on your mind.

What is the real challenge for you? This question reorients the discussion toward what the student believes is their influence on the situation and what they can do to affect it. The last two words of this question, "for you," are the most important part. They make the student assess their own ability, concentration, and interpretations, not those of others besides themselves. (Their self-comparisons to others might be discouraging them.) This line of inquiry can help the student realize that they *have* some impact. What they perceive to be the real challenge may also not be accurate or correct.

What do you want? This question might result in silence at first. For many, permission to consider what they really want might be hard to get. But this query can help the conversation move to substantial territory very quickly. In combination with the "challenge" question, this aims to get to the heart of the student and get a better idea of what their needs really are to learn and excel.

How can I help? Stainer calls this the "lazy question." That's because the teacher is having the student frame the solution they want instead of the teacher having to come up with it themselves. The teacher isn't at the point where they should be inserting their own solutions into the mix anyway—this question is designed to de-victimize the student and encourage some kind of action. It also maintains a sort of equilibrium in your relationship: the teacher isn't their savior, and the student isn't helpless. This is where the teacher learns what appears to matter to the student and what they think they are looking for.

If you're saying "yes" to this, what are you saying "no" to? This is popularly known as the "strategic" question. Executing on a decision sometimes means making choices about what to do. In deciding to take one course of action, we're effectively declining to do another. There are often opportunity costs. It's important to maintain this cognizance with the student—but it's for your own good as well, especially if you find yourself saying "yes" too much.

What was most useful to you? The final question invites the student to reflect on the exchange you've just had and what kind of emotions or declarations the questions have unlocked. This is also the point of the interaction where the key moment of insight—the "teachable moment," if you will—is most likely to be clearest and most defined. Finally, it establishes that there was value to the conversation—that is, it actually *helped*. In hindsight, what really moved the needle? Was this the same as they thought beforehand?

So consider a scenario in which each of these questions gets asked in the process of teaching and learning. Let's say a group of writers and designers is working on a major proposal to an art museum for a book about their history. The lead designer feels that there's a disconnect happening between herself and the rest of the staff and that it's impeding progress. She comes to you, the project manager, to see if there are strategic steps she can take.

"What's on your mind?" you ask. She says there's a communication gap that seems to be happening in the group. A lot of decisions are simply not being made, and still others are being assumed too quickly and not thought out well enough.

"And what else?" This is a prompt to peer a little more deeply into the situation. The lead designer might have one or two specific people in mind who are proving to be "stoppage points" in the process—or that the disconnect has been going on longer than she originally thought.

"What is the real challenge for you?" The problem is about a group of people, but this question is only for the lead herself. Maybe the challenge is that she was brought over from a different department to lead this group, and their temperament or style is difficult to get a handle on. She's wondering how she can manage them without infringing on their style or nature.

"What do you want?" The killer question— this is a direct ask that only she can answer because it's about her desired outcome. After a few seconds of completely expected silence, she says she wants to increase her group's visibility in the company. She admits part of this desire is to increase *her* personal profile as well, but not at the expense or ignorance of the individuals she's leading.

"How can I help?" You may have a solution in mind at this point—but you hold back with it.

This is, after all, a situation she has more daily knowledge of than you, so you'd like to know her opinion first. Your solution might not be appropriate after you hear her. She says she wants help in reducing the intangible barriers between team members that seem to be impeding progress. She hasn't had a lot of time to deal with these kinds of issues that don't technically reflect on the company's bottom line.

"If you're saying 'yes' to this, what are you saying 'no' to?" This question might have to be slightly rephrased, but it should address what must be sacrificed or expended in order to get what the "yes" is after. Your lead designer says she's saying 'no' to the team members operating in their own silos—or worse, an emotional vacuum.

After arriving at a plan, you ask, "What was most helpful to you?" This is the teachable moment, as mentioned above. She might say she appreciated that she could be forthright about tricky situations or that she got insight on how to approach team members with drastically different moods and methods.

This exchange shows a line of inquiry that pulls truths and awakenings from the subject but gives them control over how they're mined and revealed.

Give Good Feedback

When we learn with the intention to teach, we break the material down into simple and understandable chunks for ourselves. We're also coerced to examine the topic from a more critical, thorough standpoint to improve our comprehension. We must be able to pick actions, behaviors, and thoughts apart and steer people to the correct paths.

Delivering feedback is a key aspect in this regard. It prepares you for potential roadblocks and helps you learn in a different way. It also encourages you to work at giving honest, productive, and helpful feedback. There are a few points in the act of feedback that are important to follow:

Be specific. University of Auckland professors Helen Timperley and John Hattie stress the importance of giving learners very specific information about what they're getting right or wrong. Generalities like "Great job!" don't contain much valuable information about what the learner did right, and a vague statement like "not quite there yet" doesn't give any insight into how the student can do better next time.

Researchers, therefore, suggest taking a few extra minutes of time to give learners information about what *exactly* they did well and where they need to improve. Name the steps that made the biggest impression on you: "I liked how direct and ordered your calculations were," "You had a real command of the facts in this story," or "You seemed to get a little anxious when you talked about the numbers, but that can be fixed." It can also be of great help to tell the learner what they're doing differently than before.

Sooner is better. Feedback is always more effective when it's given as immediately as possible rather than days, weeks, or months later. One study that compared delayed versus immediate feedback showed a very significant performance increase among those who got instant assessments. Another project from the University of Minnesota showed that students who received lots of prompt feedback were better able to understand the material they'd just read.

Delayed feedback creates a psychological distance between the end of an activity and the learning moment, and that time lapse can only weaken the impact of the feedback. Better to negotiate with your schedule and ensure that your suggestions and opinions will be at their most conveyable and understood.

Tie it to a goal. Timperley and Hattie note that effective feedback is most often oriented around a specific achievement that students are working toward. Your feedback should be clearly understood in terms of how it will help students progress toward their final objective. "This essay should be an integral part of your final project," "Your layering is getting you closer to a cosmetology license," and so forth. It's encouraging to have reminders of what you are ultimately working toward.

Be careful. Your feedback has to be given in a manner that encourages rather than discourages. Some people are far more sensitive to negative feedback than others, and there's never a point in having others feel denigrated or ashamed. You have to give feedback in a way that doesn't make people fear hearing from you.

In other words, sometimes you'll have to sugarcoat your response. It's not easy to walk the line between honest and helpful. In moments of giving feedback, try to imagine how you'd want to hear it if you were in a state of only moderate confidence.

Positive feedback stimulates the brain's reward centers, leaving the recipient open to taking a new direction. Negative feedback, on the other hand, indicates that adjustment must be made, which turns on defensive instincts.

This doesn't mean you have to avoid negative or corrective feedback entirely. Just make sure it's presented respectfully and follow it up with suggested solutions and outcomes. "I'm aware you're having troubles with this part of the lesson, but I'm very confident you have the resources to break through your resistance" or "Mistakes are all part of this process, and everybody's made them—and we've all come out the other end just fine."

Finish with a plan. At the end of your feedback session, make sure there's a blueprint of actionable steps to move forward with. Without them, there's not much of a purpose to your feedback. A plan to set your guidelines in motion creates a positive, even optimistic resolution that both parties can look forward to. "Now that you've gotten through this, let's go slower on the next proposal and measure each part of it against our criteria."

Getting Feedback from Others

Finally, what about us? The prospect of hearing feedback can be a source of stress, which is why it can be difficult to ask for it. However, the more we take the initiative and ask for feedback, the less stressful it gets. Even more deeply, if we ask for honest, unsparing, or even negative feedback— "C'mon, give it to me straight"—studies show that we stand a higher chance of personal satisfaction and an ability to adapt more quickly to new roles and responsibilities.

Before asking for feedback, ask yourself what kind you're looking for. Are you seeking appreciation, evaluation of a project, or a willing mentor or coach? Don't hesitate to ask direct questions about your role—in fact, being specific and making requests like "What do I do to improve in this area?" or "How could I have handled this differently" cut past the clouds of uncertainty and get right to something real and useful.

Don't be afraid to ask for feedback too soon. In fact, just as a teacher shouldn't wait to give feedback until days after it's useful, neither should we wait to get it. Ask as close to real-time as you can get it.

Finally, widen your pool of responders. The more friends, colleagues, or online connections you request feedback from, the higher the chance that you'll be able to form a truly objective response from a multitude of perspectives. Make them feel comfortable about being direct and constructively critical. If there's one thing everyone can agree on, it's wanting to have their opinions heard!

We often think of teachers in elevated terms—which is fair, since education is a noble profession—but the best teachers would tell you they learn almost as much from their students as the students learn from them. Teaching means working with a multitude of personalities, analyzing problems, and understanding through empathy. The discoveries you make through that process can be as profound as anything you'll learn as a student. Even if you don't plan on becoming an educator, the benefits of *thinking* like one are just as accessible to you.

Takeaways to Accelerate Your Learning

1. The learning pyramid, if taken as a guideline, shows a spectrum of passive and active learning. Teaching is the most active type of learning, and thus we should seek to teach more in our quest for knowledge. When we teach, we are showing someone how to replicate behavior or actions, and if you can't do that, then your knowledge is shallower than you might think.

2. The protégé effect takes the effects of learning to the next level. It's when we feel a certain amount of responsibility, openness, and accountability because we have a protégé, which pushes us to keep striving for more and better.

3. There are seven vital questions, originally used in coaching, that you can use in teaching people to understand what they are missing, what they want, and what they are currently struggling with. Once you can understand different perspectives and struggles, you will be able to understand how to tailor your information

and also what knowledge gaps you may still possess.

4. There is an art to giving and receiving feedback. Giving feedback increases your learning because you are able to correct and instruct, thereby improving your own processes and habits. Receiving feedback increases your learning because, well, you're not always right in what you learn!

Chapter 9. Learning Habits

Habits are subconscious patterns of behavior. By definition, they don't require any thought; they're just automatic. When you try to do something that isn't a habit, you're more likely to fail. This is because it's hard to do something new while pondering the proper course of action required to do it. It's very tough to do two things at once.

Practicing and turning things into second nature allow you to accomplish more and to do so more naturally. In this chapter, we'll focus on habits that will make you better at learning and more apt to pick up on patterns and observe connections.

In a sense, habits are the ultimate expression of learning—you've learned it so well that you actually can't act or think in a different manner anymore. How do you get to this phase of learned behavior or knowledge?

Persistence

Persistence is the ability to remain focused on a task and follow through to its completion. It's sticking with a problem and refusing to let it beat you by making you give up.

Those who persist develop strategies for attacking issues even when they want to stop. They systematically try different approaches. They collect feedback to analyze what's working and what isn't. They're open to changing their approach and do so fluidly and with less disruption.

Persistence entails being comfortable with ambiguity and persevering through disappointment. People who persist are always looking for ways to achieve their goals, even when they feel motionless or stuck.

There are plenty of real-life accounts of people whose dogged persistence paid off. Walt Disney went bankrupt multiple times. Thomas Edison had 1,000 failed attempts before he successfully created the light bulb. Even Michael Jordan was cut from his high school basketball team because coaches thought he wasn't good enough. Let that sink in for a moment.

For us somewhat less renowned folks, persistence depends on some relatively easy-to-identify factors. Keeping determination as a one-track, all-encompassing attitude is great fuel. Developing a set of habits (like the ones in this chapter) help push your motivation forward when you sense it slipping. Being adjustable and flexible about your plan's execution—while maintaining your determination—is always a wise choice. Having role models to emulate—and learning how they navigated the struggles they met— is a great source of inspiration as well.

In learning, persistence means showing patience during the points where you're frustrated. It's knowing that practicing active learning *will* work when you commit. It's realizing that, by definition, trial and error are inherent parts of the education process, and it's allowing the inclusion of new approaches to solve thorny problems.

Managing impulsivity is a form of persistence and is very closely related to self-discipline. It's all about taking your time and remaining calm, thoughtful, and deliberate—and projecting that composed personality externally. Effective leaders think before they act and harness the power to deny fleeting impulses in the interests of achieving a greater goal. Instead of reacting rashly to external stimuli, they reflect on the different options available and choose the one most likely to work. As Benjamin Franklin once said, "It is easier to suppress the first desire than to satisfy all that follow it."

In the learning environment, it's about harnessing the emotional turbulence that comes from disappointment and reining in the impulse of thinking the material has defeated us. Futility can be one of the most destructive feelings we can have, making us feel like cutting our losses and dropping the effort. But we've made progress to a certain point already and need to take that into context. Retracing our steps through the material we're learning, and applying the method of self-explanation to unplug the stopping point, is an example of good impulse management.

Put in the clearest of terms, think before you act. The big picture of what you're trying to accomplish should always hover overhead. Use that overarching vision to help you decide whether a sudden, new action will truly support your aims or just be a distraction that might siphon off your efforts.

Flexible Thinking

The ability to look at problems from several different angles and perspectives is invaluable in almost any undertaking. People who are mentally flexible have the ability to consider multiple points of view. They can change their minds more readily when they get additional data or reasoning contrary to their original conclusion.

Forethought and imagination are the surest tools in developing flexible thinking. Consider the range of possible outcomes—extreme optimism and total pessimism—and imagine the results of both. Those results almost certainly won't be what happen, but be open to shifting your perspective on that scale to account for all possibilities.

Develop the trait of standing in someone else's shoes, and try to develop an objective outlook based on that viewpoint. You might have an insatiable desire for seaweed-flavored snacks—but would passersby be interested in coming to your seaweed-only bistro? (And if not, how can you *make* them interested?)

Try to overcome personal bias or the need to have definitive answers immediately. Also, account for the fleeting nature of feelings and emotions—if you're feeling hopeless that you'll never develop a skill or task you need, recognize that this feeling will dissipate the more you work on it. Flexible thinking is a product of the long view, not the quick fix.

In learning, we use flexible thinking the same way we use self-explanation: to determine alternate ways to solve problems. This could be using the scientific method to analyze a passage in literature or observing a math problem through the use of metaphor (which we'll discuss shortly). If you're really short on ideas, you can utilize the alphabet—there are 26 prompts for ideas just waiting for you (one idea beginning with each letter of the alphabet).

Striving for Accuracy

"Measure twice, cut once." The old maxim is, like most old maxims, very true. Striving for accuracy minimizes your chances of making critical mistakes: learning the rules, checking for errors, and paying attention to detail. This is how to ensure that learning is done correctly without picking up bad habits or running with misinformation.

The flip-side of that effort is that you'll develop a sense of pride and a reputation for excellence in your work. People who strive for accuracy set high standards and are always searching for new ways and techniques to master their craft.

When you're preparing a budget, use multiple sources to answer the same equation. If you're writing a piece on historical events, get confirmation on your timelines from as many sources as possible (at least three). And of course, if you're making clothes or a wood cabinet, well, measure twice and cut once. Just make sure you're correct, take pride in it, and take the long road.

Striving for accuracy almost means avoiding shortcuts. Your personal learning experience is what really matters. Even if you know you can find the answer to an exercise from a friend or on the Internet, step back and put your mental process to work.

That doesn't mean you can't ask others for help or Google the occasional news article. But always put your personal learning development as the foremost goal in your mind. Your friends may have certain opinions that color their stories, and the Internet— well, this might shock you—but sometimes the Internet isn't totally trustworthy.

Get what you need to study better and find your own answers. Keep a list of your "reliable sources" and research the reputation of new ones. And don't be afraid to question your own findings—if you still have the instinct that something in your term paper or Baked Alaska recipe is a bit off, there's probably a good reason.

In learning, we can strive for accuracy by recalculating a trigonometry equation multiple times, possibly using different methods. We verify the reliability of the news sites we visit for political science class. We ensure that all the tools and measures we use in woodworking are in good condition and properly calibrated. It's a simple matter of ensuring quality control the way professionals do.

Questioning and Posing Problems

That leads us to the more general act of challenging ourselves and our beliefs. Questioning is having an inquisitive attitude, and problem-posing involves conjuring obstacles you'd rather not think about.

"What evidence do I have that aliens landed in New Mexico?" "Am I assuming that the pursuit of happiness is an inalienable right, or did I read that wrong?" "What if I let the pressure in my car tires go below 20 psi?" "What other alternatives are there to bankruptcy?" "How can I make this the best Baked Alaska ever?"

Self-examination is never a weakness—it's as valuable of a skill to your growth and development as inventory-taking is to a business. Confronting ourselves is an anticipatory act for confronting outside challenges; it's real-world preparation we can do in the privacy of our own home. You might also recognize this general approach as skepticism or simply planting seeds of doubt and never quite believing what you're hearing until it is verified and proven.

In education, the value of questioning is self-apparent, but the relationship dynamic might inhibit a student from challenging an instructor's version of a story or a procedure. But teachers admire curiosity from the students they're teaching, as it's proof that you're activating your mind for understanding the subject as thoroughly as possible.

Were the perceived heroes and villains of a certain historical war *really* as good and bad as they're made out to be? Were cubist painters *really* that resistant to naturalism? Are there *really* no positive strategies aspiring news writers can take from yellow journalism? Whether you're questioning a person or a textbook, cross-examining an established precept—even if that precept turns out to be right—will always deepen our comprehension of the big picture.

Think in Metaphors

Metaphors, allegories, and analogies are crucial parts of the approach to learning faster. Although metaphors come from literature, ironically, they work better with technical subjects like math, chemistry, physics, and finance. That's because those subjects tend to be very abstract—so understanding their concepts requires a bit of creative representation. If you can make a metaphor about a mathematical proof, you've done the difficult task of expressing something complex in simpler terms.

When Einstein explained the theory of relativity, he used the image of himself atop a moving light beam while holding a mirror to his face. Charles Darwin explained his theory on the origin of species using the image of a branching tree. U.S. Presidents have likened our struggles to mountains, our resiliency to armies, and our rebirth to springtime. Metaphors are familiar canvases capable of explaining our big ideas (kind of like this sentence). They wield a representative power that communicates with a broad range of people.

Metaphors are also in line with a recurring idea in this book: applying past knowledge to new situations. This is basically learning from experience and being able to make sound analogies that apply that understanding in a new context. We're again pulling preexisting concepts *out* of our brains and refreshing them with new meaning. Hopefully, metaphors help our listeners and readers do that, too.

I always recommend brainstorming for metaphors. Start with open-ended questions that lead to analogies:

- "This idea reminds me of . . ."

- "I've seen this idea in real-life situations, such as . . ."

- "A phenomenon that mimics this idea is . . ."

- "If I told a story about this idea, it would go like . . ."

In general, habits may be regarded more in terms of harm than good—they're perceived somewhat as helpless addictions that are sometimes dangerous. But effective learning *loves* habits that are good and that reinforce our self-discipline while allowing space for new ideas and thoughts. Habits can support who we are; they don't erase it. And it's never too late to start a good one.

Takeaways to Accelerate Your Learning

1. The habit of persistence and discipline is key to learning because learning is not always easy or pleasurable. The ability to keep going when you'd rather do anything else will get you where you want to be. Similarly, you must learn to manage your impulsivity and resist distractions.

2. The habit of flexible thinking will allow you to consider multiple perspectives and not become married to one method, mindset, habit, or opinion. This allows you to broaden your horizons and learn.

3. The habit of striving for accuracy is self-evident. You have to make sure what you are learning is correct, and you must verify it yourself instead of relying on the words of others.

4. The habit of asking questions and skepticism will serve you well because it is a sense of genuine curiosity that will allow you to go deeper than others in learning topics and skills. Simply asking "why" continually will get you farther than you might expect.

5. The habit of thinking in metaphors is the ability to break down an idea into components and compare it to something related. It necessarily involves understanding your topics on a deeper level and applying what you already know to new knowledge.

Summary Guide

Chapter 1. Fertile Conditions to Learning

- The human attention span is significantly shorter than you would ever assume, so you must cater to it by learning in smaller blocks of time. You must also factor rest and recovery time into your learning because, like an athlete, this is where the difference is made

- Seek to prioritize underlying concepts over information. Rote memorization is rarely the most helpful kind of learning. If you learn underlying concepts first, the information can actually be predicted to some degree.

- Fail, struggle, and be frustrated. It's this type of fixation that makes cements information and concepts into your memory. In essence, taking the hard way and avoiding the shortcut is how effective learning takes place. The shortcut creates learned helplessness.

Chapter 2. Memory Retention

- Memory is what we are trying to change when we learn, and it is composed of encoding, storage, and retrieval. There are numerous pitfalls in each of those stages that sabotage our learning.

- We use our memories by recalling, recognizing, or relearning information, but we also have to contend with the forgetting curve as coined by Ebbinghaus, which documents the rate of memory decay without further rehearsal.

- Retrieval practice is the most effective method to improve our memories and thus learning, and it is exemplified by simple flashcards, which prompt for information in a vacuum without any other hints. There are numerous ways you can apply this in your daily life and numerous ways you can prompt for information

Chapter 3. Active Learning Techniques

- Passive learning activities like summarization and simple highlighting have been proven as ineffective. If you want to learn, you must engage your mind in an active manner. This is more difficult, so understandably it is done less.

- Elaborative interrogation is the process of explaining concepts to yourself and acting like Sherlock Holmes to understand what is involved in any concept. "Why" and "how" questions tend to work the best.

- Self-explanation is the process of talking out loud to yourself to discover what you know and don't know. The Feynman technique is a special application of this technique where you are able to discover blind spots based on how well you can use self-explanation with any given concept.

- Interleaved practice is the act of mixing up your subjects of study as opposed to learning subject by subject in segregated blocks. This works because you grow stronger associations and links to various information.

Chapter 4. Spaced Repetition; No Cramming

- Spaced repetition is the mother of effective learning, but sometimes that's impractical in daily life. Adjust your focus onto frequency over duration in general, and your learning will improve by leaps and bounds.
- Cramming is sometimes unavoidable, but you can still implement spaced repetition into smaller periods of time. You can also use interleaved practice and concept learning to speed up your learning.
- Flashcards and mnemonics are helpful to learning as much as possible in a short period of time because they are effective at organizing information and breaking it into chunks.

Chapter 5. Make Learning Secondary

- Learning by itself is not enough to motivate most people most of the time. That's perfectly natural. The task then becomes to find relevance, meaning, and motivation in an end goal where learning is part of the process. You can design tasks around what you have to learn to make learning secondary.

- The concept of gamification is another way to make learning secondary, as the game mechanics and progress indicators become primary—for example, level-ups, badges, rewards, etc. A powerful form of gamification comes in the form of competition and social pressure and comparison.

Chapter 6. Mistakes in Learning

- What kind of mindset do you hold toward learning? Do you have a fixed mindset, or do you have a growth mindset? You want to ensure you have a growth mindset because that is the simple belief that you can learn and can improve. Check your internal monologue and change your language to change your mindset.

- Don't fall into the myth that learning styles actually make a difference. They may appear logical, but information is information. Don't sell yourself short and miss out on information presented through various media.

- When you attempt to learn anything, you are trying to integrate it into your brain's organizational structures and methods. To do this, you must learn how to take great notes to help yourself, and the Cornell method is perfect for that. On a more general note, the more effort you put into learning something, the greater staying power it will have.

Chapter 7. Building Expertise

- Expertise is a natural consequence of learning. Ericsson stated that you simply need 10,000 hours of practice, but this wasn't quite accurate. You actually need hours of deliberate practice, which is when your only goal is to improve performance. This fundamentally changes how you rehearse because you are only as strong as your weakest link.

- The Dreyfus model of skill acquisition documents how we gain expertise and what we tend to do at each of the five stages along the way. Similarly, the four stages of competency model describes how we feel about our behaviors and habits on the road to expertise. When you can identify where you are in each of these models, you'll know what you need to do next.

- The Pareto principle is otherwise known as the 80/20 rule because in just about every walk of life, 20% of what the input will produce 80% of the output. This is easily seen in language acquisition, where knowing 100 words has been said to impart the power to recognize 50% of most sentences.

Chapter 8. Teaching to Learn

- The learning pyramid, if taken as a guideline, shows a spectrum of passive and active learning. Teaching is the most active type of learning, and thus we should seek to teach more in our quest for knowledge. When we teach, we are showing someone how to replicate behavior or actions, and if you can't do that, then your knowledge is shallower than you might think.

- The protégé effect takes the effects of learning to the next level. It's when we feel a certain amount of responsibility, openness, and accountability because we have a protégé, which pushes us to keep striving for more and better.

- There are seven vital questions, originally used in coaching, that you can use in teaching people to understand what they are missing, what they want, and what they are currently struggling with. Once you can understand different perspectives and struggles, you will be able to understand how to tailor your information and also what knowledge gaps you may still possess.

- There is an art to giving and receiving feedback. Giving feedback increases your learning because you are able to correct and instruct, thereby improving your own processes and habits. Receiving feedback increases your learning because, well, you're not always right in what you learn!

Chapter 9. Learning Habits

- The habit of persistence and discipline is key to learning because learning is not always easy or pleasurable. The ability to keep going when you'd rather do anything else will get you where you want to be. Similarly, you must learn to manage your impulsivity and resist distractions.

- The habit of flexible thinking will allow you to consider multiple perspectives and not become married to one method, mindset, habit, or opinion. This allows you to broaden your horizons and learn.

- The habit of striving for accuracy is self-evident. You have to make sure what you are learning is correct, and you must verify it yourself instead of relying on the words of others.

- The habit of asking questions and skepticism will serve you well because it is a sense of genuine curiosity that will allow you to go deeper than others in learning topics and skills. Simply asking "why" continually will get you farther than you might expect.

- The habit of thinking in metaphors is the ability to break down an idea into components and compare it to something related. It necessarily involves understanding your topics on a deeper level and applying what you already know to new knowledge.

Made in the USA
San Bernardino,
CA